MW01292440

My Name is Jirko

GEORGE BEYKOVSKÝ

DEDICATION

This book is dedicated to my dear family that I truly love. May you always stand up to racism. Love Jirko

CONTENTS

INTRODUCTION

I was born Juraj Harry Beykovský on August 22, 1931, to a Jewish family on the farm called Sabatka Puszta, near the town Rimavska Sobota, located in Slovakia. I was called Jirko, renamed Jorge when we moved to Ecuador and now in the USA I'm called George. I have one sibling, a younger brother named Tomas, born in 1936. As far as I remember, at home, I was never told of my Jewish heritage but after my parents died, I become briefly involved with other Jewish people in Seattle and I discovered my Jewish heritage. This book tells the story of my family's experience of racism as Jewish people.

JIRKO, GABY, VIKTOR AND TOMY

At the end of World War 1, the Czechs and Slovaks were brought together to form the country called Czechoslovakia - my birth country. It was made up of 50 percent Czech, 22 percent German, 16 percent Slovak, 5 percent Hungarian, 4 percent Ukrainian and small amounts of Yiddish, Polish and Hebrew. Many Czechoslovakia Jews, like myself, had lived in Prague since the eleventh century.

The country was known for its diverse population that had a democratic parliament and was the most prosperous and politically stable country in Eastern Europe, until 1938. This all changed when the racist Nazi Germans invaded and occupied the country until 1945. It's estimated these Germans killed 263,000 Jews who lived in my home of Czechoslovakia. Afterwards the Soviets took control of the country from 1945 to 1989.

The Jews killed in the Holocaust included fifty-one of my relatives who were deported to Terezin (also called Theresienstadt) a camp which served as a holding pen for Jews before being transported to the Nazi-run killing centers between 1941 and 1945.

CHAPTER 1

THE TOWN OF UHŘÍNĚVES

The Beykovský family farm was named Pitcovitz and is located near the town Uhříněves. Uhříněves is also called Prague 22, and is a municipal district near the city of Prague, in the country now called Czechia. The administrative district comprises municipal districts Prague 22, Benice, Kolovraty, Královice and Nedvězí.

The Synagogue building where my family attended still exists, located in the south eastern part of Prague. In days past, passengers traveled back and forth between Prague and Uhříněves by daily train or by horse and carriage, but in modern day, the town is only a twenty minute journey from each other by car or public transportation.

The Beykovský family lived in this Jewish community in the town of Uhříněves for centuries, according to information obtained from the Czech Archives. My oldest known relative was Samuel Beykovský, who was born in 1719, and was the father of Bernard and the father of Jacub, and is my great great-grand-father, before the farm of Pitcovitz existed. I travelled all over the world to find my relatives, my records now contain nine generations of Beykovský. When I started gathering information in 1995, I began with only the name of my grandfather Gustav, and his offspring of three generations.

Hugo Gold, a renowned Czech historian, includes a chapter on Uhříněves in his book "The Jews and Jewish Communities in

Bohemia", circa 1934. The chapter is titled TOWARDS THE HISTORY OF THE JEWS IN UHRINEVES NEAR PRAGUE, compiled by Jaroslav Polak-Rokycana". This relates to my ancestors and mentions my great grandfather Jacob Beykovský. Here is an excerpt:

> "Until the year 1817, the Jews who lived in Uhříněves came together for communal prayer in a private home which originated from the year 1810. Only after 1848 could the community, which was greatly augmented, planned the construction of a dignified synagogue in city plot #79 and to this purpose public collections took place. When completed the prayer house contained 48 seats for men and 27 for women, next door exists a flat of the teacher or the cantor, which consists of two rooms and a kitchen. The upper floor contains a large room for meetings, and antechamber and an attic. The membership was entered into a special book in the synagogue related to the seats, and connected to the contributions of the members. For example: Josef Beykovský bought in the year 1862 the men's seat number 1 and the women's seat number 2 for 50 Gulden and ensured this with a contribution for upkeep of 3 Gulden yearly. Jacub Beykovský bought in the year 1863 the men's seat number 2 to number 9 and the women's seat number 3 for 94 Gulden."

On September 18, 1999, I was invited to visit the Finchley Reform Synagogue in London, England, and the morning services for Shabbat. This memorial is to commemorate the Jews from Uhříněves who were transported by train to the Terezin Nazi camp, in 1942. Approximately 250 people attended the memorial service.

In WWII many synagogues (buildings) were destroyed, but this one in Uhříněves was spared, probably because this synagogue was in disuse. At the same time, hundreds of Torah were confiscated by the Nazis and shipped to a museum in Germany.

For those who don't know, the Torah is the first section or first five books of the Jewish bible. It's written in Hebrew, the oldest of Jewish languages and is also known as Torat Moshe, or the Law of Moses.

After the war, the Torah were entrusted to a Jewish organization for safekeeping and distribution. The Torah that were in good condition (Kosher) were entrusted to Synagogues that did not have financial means to buy one, and others were given to museums. The Finchley synagogue received one of these Torahs. Members of this synagogue continue to commemorate this event on the same date yearly.

For me, the most important and rewarding part of the ceremony was to hold in my arms the Torah that originally belonged to the Uhříněves Synagogue. I was honored to hold in procession the same Torah that in last century Jacub, Josef and Wilem Beykovský possibly held for their prayers. The memorial at Finchley was held partly in Hebrew, partly in Czech and partly in English.

Synagoga (vnějšek)

THE SYNAGOGUE THEN AND NOW

Many of the Jews deported to the Terezin camp are listed in the program. Very few of those deported survived. My cousin Hanna Fuchs was one of the holocaust survivors from the concentration camps and she continued to live with one of her children in Prague, Czech Republic. Sadly, Hanna died of old age on April 16, 2018, in Prague.

I was aware of Hanna but did know if she still was still alive, until in 2000, when I put an ad in a German periodical that is dedicated to those who survived concentration camps searching for family connections. One year later I was fortunate to make contact with Hanna, thanks to someone in Australia who recognized the name, who connected me to someone in Los Angeles, who gave me an address in

עץ חיים היא

JIRKO HOLDING THE FAMILY TORAH

Boston, Massachusetts.

At last in 2001, for my 70th birthday, Hanna and her son Michael come to my home in Everett, Washington, and we celebrated meeting for the first time, ever, and to celebrate my birthday. Hanna gave a precious present for my birthday, two pieces of linen from 1860, that

MEETING MATTHEI, HANNA, AVERY AND JOE

belonged to my great grandmother's trousseaux. These two handkerchiefs have the letters "LD" hand-embroidered for Louise Dubsky. She was the wife of my great-grandfather Josef Beykovský. Hanna and I have in common our great-grand father Josef Beykovský and therefore Hanna is my cousin.

In 1996, Karel Bejkovský (at that time we did not yet know of a family connection between his and mine) drove me around Uhříněves where we visited the cemetery, the synagogue, the location where Beykovský's farmed and to the home of Mr. Tingle who worked as a youngster at the Beykovský farm. Karel was instrumental in my success researching archives in Prague, and finding many of my ancestors. Records show my ancestors were among the important figures of the Uhříněves Jewish Community:

- Josef Beykovský (my great grandfather) was the first chairman of the community 1893-1901, and
- Wilhelm (Vilem) Beykovský (his brother) was treasurer 1901-1919. Vilem was a farmer and owned an estate in Pitcovice a nearby hamlet.

We were quite sad and disappointed on our visit to the cemetery with overgrown vegetation, unkept for years, very few tombstones were erect and many were missing. Of course we did not locate where Vilem and other Beykovský family were buried. Karel and I visited the office of the Jewish organization that maintains cemeteries in that country and informed us there were no records available. They also mentioned that many of the more modern marble tombstones were robbed and used for foundations or in decorating buildings. The cemetery contains several other tombstones dating back to 1730. The Uhříněveská Jewish community ceased to exist in 1940 due to the holocaust.

In Uhříněves, Mr. Tingle, who is now totally blind, told us about working as a handy man at the Beykovský farm where they raised horses of excellent quality and grew wheat and other grains to feed animals. He remembered Vilem and Louise having three children: Anna, Frantisek and Hanus. He said the mother and boys were taken to Terezin concentration camp and a local policeman told Mr. Tingle that one of the boys was shot to death. A few weeks after I arrived back at my home in USA, I received a photograph that included Frantisek and Hanus Beykovský, from the daughter of Mr. Tingle.

BEYKOVSK PITCOVITZ FARM HOUSE

Both Pitcovitz as well as Uhříněves are names that appear in many documents about the family but are both of the same location and it's

Uhříněves Cemetery - old section.
Photos by Karel Bejkovsky - 2004.

my conclusion that the farm's name of Pitcovitz was near the Jewish community Uhříněves in the administrative district called Ricanyi.

CHAPTER 2

MY MOTHER'S STORY

GABRIELE BEYKOVSKÝ (NEE KENDE)

1901-1994, FROM INNSBRUCK AUSTRIA TO ECUADOR

GABY'S CHILDHOOD 1901-1920

All three of my sisters told me that they saw the stork fly by while they were at dinner, moments after my father announced that another sister had been born. I was born Gabriele Kende or Gaby for short. It was the 12th of September in the year 1901. My eldest sister Ilona was nine, Margit was eight and Dora four. I imagine that these days it's difficult to understand that children of those ages, during that period, still believed in the stork, but that's the way it was.

When my father told his friends that he had another girl, they all said, "Poor chap, he's got four daughters." But he replied, "It doesn't matter -when girls marry, their parents gain a son." And the truth of it was that each son-in-law would prove to be like a son to my parents.

First, let me tell you what I know of my parents. My father Ignaz Kende, born 1862, was a young "self-made man". He was from Hungary and worked in the grain business dealing in wheat, barley, oats, and corn and so on, most of it bought in Hungary and sold in other parts of Moravia, Austria and Hungary. He lived in Vienna and sold oats to the Army for its horses. At that time it was a big thing to do business with the Army. I'm told that one day he delivered a shipment of oats that weren't in very good condition, and a General said to him, "Imagine, Mr. Kende, if this had happened in time of war..." My father replied with a straight face, " You would have lost the war."

My father's parents, his two brothers and two sisters lived in Hungary. The name of the city was Nagy- Kanisza and was near a lovely lake called Balaton. (I'll tell you of that region a bit later). All that I know of my father is what I've been told, because tragically he died when I was barely two and a half. He must have been a cultured

GABY'S FATHER IGNAZ KENDE

and cultivated man, with a special sense of humor. I've had many of his "boons most" repeated to me.

Father looked Hungarian -not very tall, dark hair and dark eyes. My sister Ilona resembled him. Margit had curly, chestnut-colored hair, and green eyes. One eye had a coffee colored spot, something rather rare. Dora had blond hair with big waves in it, and light-colored eyes. And I, well you already know me.

We lived in Innsbruck, Austria. My parents had good friends there. All were Jews since in those times people usually had friends from the same religion, even though no one was very religious. There was no Jewish registry in Innsbruck, so they had to register us in another city in the Tyrol where there was a rabbinate.

Mother told me once that Father had a tumor in the base of his spinal column and that it was believed to be the result of a fall from a tree when he was young. Who knows? He died at forty two, of melanoma of the kidneys, but managed during his short life to make a lot of money, leaving a good dowry for each of us, and my mother well provided for.

When she was left a widow Mother decided to move closer to her mother in Olmütz (now known in Czech as Olomouc), about an hour's train ride from Hohenstadt. At that time the province of Moravia was a possession of the Austro-Hungarian Empire. Mother was born and raised in Hohenstadt. The city was small but the paternal house was a large one. Her father had a distillery, a liqueur factory and a farm. The Fröhlich family, were like nobles of that time, Jewish, appreciated and respected for their goodness and honor. My grandfather Albert and his wife Betty had six daughters and three sons. My mother Emmy was the fourth daughter. (Grandmother actually gave birth to thirteen children but only nine lived.)

Family life was like that of the nobility, based on respect and culture. The eldest son inherited the factory and the farm. When Grandfather died the two eldest daughters were already married and had their own children. Initially Grandmother ran the businesses on her own as her eldest son, my Uncle Julius, was still not trained to carry a business.

I won't describe the house in Hohenstadt much since my sister Dora has already written about it in much detail. But I still remember my grandmother as she reigned over the employees, and can see her allotting twice daily the milk for sale from the farm. Our vacations there were always memorable. The Fröhlich had beautiful horses, some of which were only for drawing the coaches which were driven by a uniformed coachman with "F' engraved in his buttons.

When Mother was fourteen she was sent to a boarding school in Dresden, Germany. The city was known for schools to which wealthy

GABY AND HER MOTHER EMA

people sent their daughters to perfect their foreign languages (in Mother's case French), to see the famous museums, and to learn history and literature. One side of the family, a brother and sister of my grandfather, lived in Vienna and one day when my mother was visiting them, she met my father. Apparently it was "love at first sight" and my father later traveled to Hohenstadt to ask for Emmy's hand. Like all of the daughters, my mother was married in the paternal house. After the wedding she and Father moved to Innsbruck.

Mother was a truly exceptional person, it's hard to describe fully such a special personality. My bed was in the same room as her writing desk and I remember waking up occasionally thinking it was morning when in reality Mother was still awake writing letters. I hardly ever saw her cry or complain about the hard task of raising four daughters by her self. It seems to me that because I had never really known my father, I was treated with some special tenderness. She said that I was very much like him and that we would have got on well. I remember some tears escaped her when I asked why I couldn't have a little brother, something I wanted very much.

I was a quiet child. I liked to play alone with small dolls, and never looked much for company. Dora was closest to me in age and frequently was my playmate. But she was always very lively and Mother had problems with her, which was not the case with me. I believe that she never had to punish me, and only once had to say to me, "If you keep doing that I'll send you to bed without your supper." When suppertime came around they looked for me and when I didn't appear, they finally realized that I was already in bed sleeping. I wasn't really that interested in food.

Since I was born in September my birthday was at the beginning of the school year. I began at exactly six years of age. By law we had to attend classes in religion, and one of my first questions was, " If a loving God exists, why did he let my father die?" My mother was a very liberal person, possibly agnostic, and didn't make us attend religious occasions or go to synagogue. But we had to go to religion classes in school.

From a very young age I was interested in flowers. In Hohenstadt I spent many hours with the gardener and learnt a lot from him. I also loved to look after children, and when one of my aunts had her first grandson I would go every day after school to look after him. I was a constant companion to my mother when we went out to stroll in the lovely parks, or visiting, or shopping. I was very impressed with myself when we would return to the house and Mother would ask me how much money we had spent and where we'd spent it. She couldn't remember but I could, every cent that we'd spent. So I'd help her do her accounts, which she kept in a notebook.

Once a year Uncle Julius would come from Hohenstadt to do a balance sheet. Mother had enough money and it seems she administered it correctly because my uncle said to her, "…you've handled your money very well." During his annual visit the dining room would be full of smoke something which impressed us, we left him alone to work in peace. Since there were six women in the house, Mother, the four daughters and a maid, it was a special occasion to have a man in the house for a day. From the time my sisters were small until I was twelve, we had a "mademoiselle" living with us to teach us French, which we all spoke very well. My mother read many books in French and spoke it with great perfection.

In school I was neither a very good student nor a bad one, passing easily from grade to grade. I never had very intimate friends but I was friendly with everyone and made them laugh with jokes I told quietly, so the teacher never knew why the students were laughing.

We spent the long vacations in the Tyrol, near Innsbruck or around Olmütz. Frequently we found ourselves with cousins. My Aunt Anna was the closest in age to our Mother, and like her, was widowed quite young and had four children. Marianne, one of the daughters, was around the age of Dora and cousin Gerhardt was my age (40 years later, Gerhardt and his wife and three daughters disappeared; possibly they ended their days in a concentration camp). We spent some lovely vacations together and liked each other very much. We were pretty good kids and we invented games to play. We also collected mushrooms in the woods, and strawberries, blueberries and butterflies in meadows.

During the school vacations of 1914, I was in the Tyrol once again with my mother when the First World War broke out. When we got back to Olmütz we found that all the young men had enlisted as soldiers and my sister Margit, who had always been interested in medicine, was working as a volunteer nurse in a military hospital that had been set up in a barracks. I set myself the task of keeping a garden around the hospital, and they called me a "volunteer gardener." I often spent hours waiting in lines to buy food, and for this one needed ration cards to receive a certain amount of bread, flour, potatoes and so on. I remember that Mother made a bean pie that used powdered eggs. Sometimes I would take a basket to Hohenstadt to fetch some vegetables or potatoes that they had in the garden.

As my sister Ilona was quite a bit older than I, she felt more like my mother than my sister. She loved to cook and was always making wonderful cakes, letting me lick the dough off the bowl when she baked. She also did beautiful handiwork and finally left for Vienna to study photography. Margit was completely different, although she was only eleven months younger than Ilona. It was said that she always lived in the clouds, dreaming of a great career in medicine. She studied nursing and worked as a nurse after the war. Dora at first took a secretarial course. When she finished it Mother sent her to Berlin to a school where they taught the administration of institutions such as sanatoria and hospitals.

When it came my turn to choose a profession, the War had broken out. After the war there was no money for my continued education since Mother, on the advice of Uncle Julius, had put all of her money and that of her daughters in the famous war bonds. Patriotism had come to the point where everyone felt an obligation to lend money to the State. But Austro-Hungary lost the war, and with it the majority of the money. My mother's younger brother Oskar lived in Zagreb, Yugoslavia, where he had a lovely farm, forests and a lumber business. He lived alone after having been divorced, and urged my mother to come with Dora and me to live with him. So we went to Yugoslavia and spent an agreeable period without cold or hunger from 1918 till 1920.

I think it was in 1916 that some relatives invited me to Hungary, and I made my first trip. I was 15 at the time. It was quite a big adventure for a teenager to travel by herself. Naturally I traveled all the way by train since there weren't any other means of transport. I found Hungary to be a totally different country, all the customs were new to me. First I went to Nagy-Kanisza where my father was buried. His sister Hermine was married to a Mr. Armuth, and they had a delicatessen and food shop. They also opened the first cinema in the city, and it was great fun for me to enter for free, sitting first in the front rows and then in the back. A pianist who played whatever he felt like to be appropriate to the action on the screen accompanied the film.

Even though the war was on there was an abundance of food. Hungarian cooking is very rich everything is cooked with cream or sour cream. Lunch often included two meat courses and there was always wine. Aunt Hermine also had a hotel next to the lovely lake Balaton Bereny, not one building but a number of bungalows. They also had huge vineyards and the surrounding countryside was spectacularly beautiful. The different sizes and colors of grapes were so impressive to me, as I've never seen anything like them.

From there I traveled further south to Slovenia where another of my father's sisters lived, in a part of what is now Yugoslavia. Back then it was all part of the Austro-Hungarian Empire. Zagreb was the capital of Croatia and Esseg (Osijek) was the capital of Slovenia, going there was an even greater adventure. In the train station of Esseg, I waited for my cousin who was on military leave and he collected me in a coach pulled by two horses. We drove for an hour to a village called Cepin where the Biichler family lived (the wife was my father's sister). They had three sons all of whom were officers in the military, and two daughters much older than I was. Their house was very big and they had a store where they sold groceries, grain, hardware and farm equipment, fabric, cookware and lots of other things. Behind the house was a farm where my cousins raised fine horses, but since it was wartime they couldn't develop this beyond a hobby. They used to name the colts after their cousins, and I remember a photo of a colt called Gabriele.

This part of the Empire was quite far south and had a very distinct climate, warm and dry and all pasture and meadow full of grazing livestock. That is where I first saw stables with nothing more than a roof where the livestock went in the winter -in the spring they were already grazing.

The two cousins were also named Ilona and Margit, and they were always wonderful to me, treating me as the little visitor. The whole family helped in the store on market days when the villagers came in large numbers.

Now I'll go forward in time a few years, telling about the bad luck this family had following 1918. When the soldiers came back from the War, they came under the influence of revolutionaries and began to destroy anything they found in their path. They'd enter the palaces of rich aristocrats, and if the owners didn't flee in time, the soldiers would kill them, break furniture and paintings, go into the cellar and smash all the wine kegs, many of which were of fine vintage.

The house of the Büchlers was all on one floor, and the soldiers began by smashing doors and windows and finished by setting fire to the house. The parents and two daughters escaped out the back way. When the sons came back from the war they found nothing where once had been their house. All over Europe terrorism and revolution reigned. New countries emerged like Czechoslovakia and Yugoslavia; others' borders were changed such as happened in parts of Italy and Hungary.

We heard of none of those horrors while we were in the house of our uncle in Zagreb. Dora began to work in a bank, and in 1920 I went back to Olmütz. Margit had married in 1918 when her fiancé returned from the war. Ilona married a few years later after meeting her future husband in Carlsbad, where she was working in a photographic studio. He was Dr. Kohner; a man who worked all his days for the ideal of Zionism and who during his student days was a member of the Zionist Party. They had two children, Lea and Imi, who grew up with the ideals of their parents. In 1939 they would receive their honorary certificate that allowed them to enter Palestine.

But going back to 1920, my mother and I lived alone in Olmütz. Frequently I was called to Hohenstadt to look after one of my cousins. She was Betty, the last one, who was born when her parents already had four grown children. I loved being there, in the big house with its two flower- filled gardens and huge trees that had been planted in the time of my grandparents. Behind there was a garden full of fruits and vegetables and small lakes full of fish. In winter when the lakes froze over they would cut the ice and keep it all year in a cellar covered in earth and a special straw. From there the ice was taken in pieces to the kitchen where it was put in a special icebox for preserving food (that was the "refrigerator"). The garden also had a greenhouse where the gardener planted his seeds for flowers and vegetables. For me this was a paradise, and I learned a lot from the gardener. My little cousin Betty thought I was too tough on her. One day when my mother came to visit, Betty said, " Aunt Emmy, take your daughter home, she's very strict with me!"

Ida, one of my mother's younger sisters, also lived in Olmütz and was married to a Herr Wolf. He was owner of a brewery. They had four children. The oldest was Hermann who was Dora's age, and then the twins Elizabeth and Elfriede who were a year older than me. Finally there was a little sister who was born seven years after the twins. I was always friendly with the twins, and after they had to repeat a year we were in the same grade in primary school.

For me the prettiest and most emotional occasion was Christmas, which we always spent with the Wolfs. Since in winter it started to get dark by four in the afternoon, my mother and sisters and Ida would leave for their house by that hour with a basket of presents. And the children would gather in one room to wait for the arrival of Father Christmas. When a bell rang we would jump up and run to a door of the salon, which would open and reveal the enormous tree adorned with lit candles. Then it was time for presents.

Finally at eight o'clock a delicious meal was served with the traditional fish course, a large and special carp that had been raised for the occasion. Full of happiness, surprises and the wonderful meal, we'd leave for our house.

MARRIAGE AND FAMILY, 1920-1939

Mother had a friend in Germany whom she'd met when both were holidaying in the Tyrol. For many years they wrote to each other about their respective lives. One day this woman wrote about her married son who had three children and lived in Halle an der Saale, in the province of Sachsen (Saxony). She said he was looking for a girl of good family to be their nanny, and wondered if Mother would ask me if I was interested in the job. I decided to give it a try and go there. Another country and another milieu, it sounded interesting. So I left my mother by herself January of 1924.

The father was a gynecologist, and his wife helped in his practice. The older daughter was ten years old, the second seven, and the little boy was five. I was accepted like another daughter and had my own room. I had no heavy work since there was already a cook and a maid in the house, so I concerned myself with getting the children to school, taking the little boy to the park, and so on. During school vacations we almost always traveled. I remember once going to one of the Dolomite Mountains in the southern Tyrol near Bozen. The couple also took me to the theatre, to concerts and to all kinds of interesting lectures.

I stayed with them until 1929, when I returned to our house in Olmütz. One day I saw Mother address a letter to a Mr. Viktor Beykovský. "Who is he, Mother?", I asked. I've never heard of him." She replied with what I thought was a slightly embarrassed smile, "He is a young man who is the administrator of the estate at Kocvar. I met him when I was visiting my sister Marie and he struck me as very pleasant. He's written me that his mother has died and I'm sending my condolences." And that was all we said of the matter.

The Kocvar estate was in Bohemia, between Prague and Pilsen. You went there by train and then had to travel about an hour by horse-drawn coach. Marie, the eldest of Mother's sisters, at the age of sixteen had married an estate-owner named Mändl and had lived in

Kocvar ever since. The estate-owners all knew each other and each Tuesday there was an agricultural market in Prague where they met to talk about harvests, livestock, families and so on. And that is also how they got to know about each other's children, or perhaps I should say that's how they "coordinated" marriages.

In the same spirit, every year the families of Fröhlich, Mändl, Beykovský, etc. got together at Carlsbad to take another year's cure for their livers and other troubles. (Then they spent the rest of the year eating too much rich food!) Aunt Marie had three daughters, and one of them ran the estate when her father died, though always with the help of administrators. Gustav Beykovský, another estate-owner, sent his son Viktor to get some experience at Kocvar, as he had just graduated from the agricultural university at Halle.

Mother wanted to return to Kocvar to visit her sister, and since I was now free I went along with her. That was how I met Viktor, and I believe it was "love at first sight" on both our parts. As a small child I had once declared, "I want to marry a farmer and have seven sons, and on my dining room table I want to have a bowl full of fruit from our own farm." Well, I didn't marry a farmer for that reason only...

Around that time Margit had invited me on a skiing trip to Davos, Switzerland. I had learned that wonderful sport during the years I spent in Hohenstadt, when my cousins had always taken me to the mountains. Later I often went with Margit to the Erzgebirge, a mountain range between Bohemia and Germany close to the city of Teplitz where she lived almost at the foot of the mountain. My excursions with her are unforgettable for me; with our knapsacks on our backs the two of us hiked from mountain to mountain.

It must have been already spring because when we came down from the mountains with our skis the meadows were full of little flowers, the first to appear in the spring when the snow disappears. Mother was still in Kocvar when I returned from my lovely trip, and Viktor came to the station to pick me up. He almost didn't recognize me because I was so tanned from the winter sun, which is reflected so strongly by the snow that one tans quickly to an almost bronze color.

That was the spring of 1930, and I think that Viktor and I were equally sure that we wanted to marry. One night he invited my mother and I to see "The Bartered Bride", which is the most beloved of the Czech operas. While we were in the train, with only three of us in the compartment, Mother said, "I'm going to tell you a story. You two could have been brother and sister. Viktor, your father came to our house when I was young to ask for my hand in marriage. But frankly, I didn't care for him and didn't want to marry him. So he went away and shortly after wards I met your father, Gabriele, and married him." Imagine our surprise! I replied, "That was great luck for me, Mother, it would have been sad not to have met Viktor and have him as my fiancé." We decided to marry on the 24th June 1930.

As Viktor was also Jewish but not a practicing one, we only had a civil marriage in a village near the estate. My aunt Marie was the witness on my part and uncle Vilem Beykovský was Viktor's. For our honeymoon we went to Dubrovnik, a beach resort on the Adriatic Sea in the south of Yugoslavia. When we returned the harvest had begun at the estate. At the end of it there was a beautiful Thanksgiving festivity.

The farm workers made crowns of the harvested grains, which were adorned with real and artificial flowers. One was given to the owner and another to the administrator.

We had a little apartment in the estate house, but Viktor wanted to get ahead and be independent, so he planned to lease or buy a property. At that time began the first problem of our life together, I say first because life presented us with so many more. All that I have heard of Viktor's father suggests that he was a very strict and severe man, like so many of those brought up in the machismo of their time. Everything had to run according to his orders, the way he imagined they had to be done. Long before he met me, Viktor had been seeing a working-class girl from Halle. When his father found out about it he was furious: he declared that he could no longer trust Viktor to look after his inheritance {both of Viktor's brothers had died} so there was one else to leave his possessions to. So he put it all in trust with a lawyer named Kersch who was the husband of one of Vilem's cousins, with the instruction that the inheritance would go to Viktor on the day that he married a girl of good Jewish family.

When Viktor finally tried to claim his inheritance, which was worth a million and a half Czech Krone; it turned out that Kersch had lost it all, and not only Viktor's but that of other people whose money he held in trust. Though it was never clear where the money went, it was said that he lost it on poker and playing the horses. Viktor and the others took Kersch to court and had him thrown into prison, but the little bit of money that we received from the lawsuit wasn't enough to lease even a small estate in Bohemia or Moravia.

So Viktor went to Slovakia where land was cheaper and farming methods less advanced {these days we say "underdeveloped"}, to look for a property. Uncle Vilem went with him to give his okay, and so it was that in January of 1931 we moved to the Sobota Puszta estate (Puszta is Hungarian for estate), three kilometers from the little city of Rimavska Sobota.

This whole region had belonged to Hungary until the year 1918, when it was annexed to what became Czechoslovakia. The leasing arrangement was made with the city of Rimavska Sobota.

There was a small house for us with four rooms, a kitchen and a bathroom and that was all, and no electric light or drinking water. For water there was a traditional Hungarian well. It was very deep and you had to wind a bucket down to the water with a large crank, and then wind it back up again when it was full. For light we used kerosene lamps. To one side of the patio there were huts for the farm workers as well as those of "Gazda" the estate manager and Yahuz the shepherd. On the other side there were stables for the cows and pigs and a shed for machinery and the tractor. I kept chickens and ducks, helped by a woman named "Kalafuska" who was married to one of the farm workers. In the Springtime I asked Viktor for a bit of land to grow vegetables.

But bad luck followed us. The first harvest was a disaster in the whole region. In the short time we'd been there Viktor had gained such trust with the neighbors that they asked him to go to the Ministry of Agriculture in Prague to ask for aid or a subsidy. It also helped that he was Czech and could speak more easily with the Minister than the Slovaks, who were looked down on by the Czechs.

By that time I was pregnant and the doctor calculated that the baby should be born on the 8th of August. My mother came to stay with me. When the date came and the baby hadn't appeared, Mother said, "Don't be impatient, my daughter, if the baby doesn't come now you'll have to wait another 14 days." Which is what happened. The great day came on August 22.

Ever since my childhood I had dreamed of having sons, so naturally the birth of my son was a great thing. It was probably the happiest day of my life. The midwife who attended me was a woman with a great deal of experience -I believe mine was the 780th birth of her career. Even without electric light or running water there was no problem. The only suggestion she made was that water be brought from the city to bathe the infant, so when we sent tanks of milk to the city for sale they would come back full of water. Scarcely after the birth I thanked the woman and said, "Just so you know, in two years we'll do the same business together. " She laughed heartily and said; "No one has ever said this to me before -you're something special!"

My son was born in the morning, and in the evening Viktor arrived back from a trip to Prague. One of the farm workers went to pick him up at the station, and said, " You have a son, Mr. Beykovský." It was a happy day for me. I never tired of looking at and admiring the baby. Since by that time Viktor had neither parents nor siblings, he wrote to Uncle Vilem that our son had been born on the 22nd of August. Uncle Vilem wrote back immediately that he was pleased to hear the new Beykovský had been born on August 22 because he was the fourth one from the family born on that date. Since in that part of Czechoslovakia three languages were spoken - Slovak, Hungarian and German -we thought we should give the baby a name that could be used in all three as well as Czech. We decided on Jirko (Czech), Juror (Slovak), George (German) and Guiro (Hungarian). But since Viktor was a true Czech patriot, the name that stuck was Jirko.

Viktor had suffered a lot in his childhood because at the age of ten he had been sent away to school in Prague. Looking at his child one day, Viktor said, "What luck that it won't be necessary to send him away to a big city for secondary school? We already have a high school here in Rimavska Sobota and an agricultural college. Who would have thought that Jirko would have his eighth birthday in the city of Guayaquil in Ecuador, South America?

His development was exceptional. When he was five months old I made my first trip with him to Louts, carrying him in a wicker laundry basket because it was a long trip. First we took a taxi to Lucerne and from there went for about six hours by a direct and rapid train to where my mother lived. At six months Jirko was standing in his crib, and he began to walk at ten months. He ate with such gusto that one couldn't put food into his mouth quickly enough to satisfy him. As a small child he was a charmer with his straight blond hair. Viktor's hair had been the same when he was a child. We know this because among the jewelry left by his mother there were locks of blond hair marked "Viktor." Jirko's eyes were clear blue, and he was never heard to cry!

His great friend was Gazda, the major domo. Gazda used to take Jirko with him to supervise the people working, seating him in the sowing tractor and other places where he could watch.

I kept working with my ducks and chickens, and in my vegetable garden. It was wonderful for me to see the chicks and baby ducks born in the spring. I also harvested tomatoes and cucumbers, which Kalafuska took to market to sell. She made a delicious rye bread for us, which we baked in the oven on the patio.

Almost every year in the winter I took Jirko to visit my mother. And in the summer people visited us to enjoy the good life we had on the estate. My sisters and their children visited us, and there are many photos from this period. Christmas was Viktor's favorite celebration, and we always had a tree adorned with chocolates, small red apples, and our own homemade cookies. All the rooms in the house were warmed with stoves made of clay tiles. The kerosene lamps had to be cleaned each day. If not, they gave off a black smoke that got the

Gaby & Jirko
1931

whole room dirty. Our meals were simple but abundant, made with the products of the estate: bread, milk, chicken, vegetables, lard from our pigs. Each winter we'd butcher a well-fattened pig whose meat we smoked and the lard from which would last us for months.

When Jirko was two years old I became pregnant again, and was very sad when I had a miscarriage.

The harvests got better, we lived a happy and tranquil life, and we worked hard at improving things. Since this part of Slovakia was warm, we sowed corn, tobacco and melons. The harvest and curing of the enormous leaves of tobacco was something interesting and new for us. We gave Jirko a little donkey and cart, and he quite handily helped with the harvest. He got involved in everything and was like an adult. He also occasionally went along with the shepherd when he took the sheep (about 250 of them) to pasture.

The year 1935 was a good one. The harvests in the region were abundant and Viktor was named "receiver" of grains for an agricultural society. The estate had a huge silo three stories high which seemed to be the ideal place to store the grain of all the neighboring farmers. One day my mother asked, "Viktor, don't you think it's dangerous to fill all three floors with such heavy loads of grain?" So Viktor called a neighboring engineer and asked if it was dangerous. The engineer said he didn't think so, so we kept storing grain. But catastrophe struck. One day Gazda came to us pale and trembling, telling us that the top floor had collapsed through the other two, and all the grains had got mixed in with each other. The worst of it was that the majority of the grains belonged to other farmers. I don't remember how the affair was sorted out, but it was a terrible time because Viktor was blamed and made responsible.

Despite that, I was happy because I was pregnant again and I think that may be why I don't remember many details of that unpleasant affair. "I hope it's another boy," I said, "the second of the seven I want to have." Once again Mother came to stay and the same midwife to whom I'd said that we would have the same business to do in two years. I'm told that Viktor was in a room nearby, watching a clock in order to see at what hour would come the cry of the new baby. It was the 19th of February 1936. My happiness was complete because I had another son.

Although he weighed more at birth than Jirko had, he was always a little delicate. But he was no trouble at all to raise. We gave him the name Tomas, and since my mother liked the name Ian we give him that one too. Jirko was four-and-a-half when Tomy was born.

We never inscribed either child in the Jewish registry. Viktor felt and I agreed that when they were grown they would decide if they wanted a religion. Although at that time the problems with Hitler had already started in Germany, no one could imagine that it would get worse and another world war would break out with all its cruelties.

Each year at harvest time a group of agricultural workers would arrive from a village called Klenovec which, though close by, was situated in the mountains. They traveled in primitive wagons drown by horses. The group consisted of fifteen persons and their leader contacted to bring in the harvest, being paid partly in cash and partly in kind.

The leader's name was Dovala, and he brought along his wife who cooked in a big soup cauldron. Though poor and simple, they had a great deal of what we called "the culture of the heart." Dovala was the policeman in his village and also made a living curing animal skins. He and his wife had four daughters and a son, and from the beginning they had a great deal of affection for Jirko -so much that when they finished the harvest they would take him to their village for a few days visit. I used to send even Jirko's crib along so that he'd have the comfort he was accustomed to at home. He went many times, adapting well to the primitive household and enjoyed himself with the five children who made much of him. He got his milk from Mrs. Dovala's goat, and often went down to the stable with Gazda looking for some job to do. Once he cut his foot but kept on running around barefoot without worrying about the wound, causing my sister Dora to say, "The tetanus germs run away when they see Jirko coming."

GABY, TOMY AND JIRKO - 8/1936

The years passed, and we heard of terrible things happening in Germany under the infamous Hitler. He invented Nazism, saying that he was going to rid Germany of all those who weren't Nazis or of German stock. He was against Catholics, but the worst was his persecution of the Jews. N o one ever understood why he hated Jews so much, but it's said that he chose them to show the Germans how well things would be in the country when it was one hundred percent German.

While Tomy was still very small, the children of relatives sometimes came to spend the summer vacation with us at the estate. We all had a lot of fun. Margit's youngest son Hans and Ilona's son lmi spent some weeks with us.

The harvests were good and if we hadn't had our political worries we would have lived a happily untroubled life. The cattle and sheep increased and we sowed tobacco, keeping within a quota authorized and controlled by the government. I too earned a fair amount of money selling vegetables, fattened ducks, and above all eight-week old piglets. Viktor had given me a lovely purebred sow who was pink and produced litters twice a year. She always gave birth to large litters, the largest of which had eighteen piglets. Kalafuska's wife went to the fair to sell the piglets, and when I asked her how sales were going she replied, "Don't tell me to lower the price I'm selling them for!" Because she knew I always felt sorry for people who looked poor and wanted to buy one.

THE GERMAN OCCUPATION

I spent the winter with my sons at my mother's house in Olmutz, some days by ourselves and others with Viktor. There we heard more about what was going on in Germany, but we never thought that the plague of Hitlerism would reach us. Jirko had begun first grade in the school at Rimskva Sobota. Sometimes he went on his bicycle and other times he was taken in a wagon. Viktor and I also had bicycles, and we enjoyed making little outings on them.

Thus arrived March of 1938, and the Germans occupied Austria. This was serious matter for Czechoslovakia, since the menace Hitler was coming ever closer. Then in September 29-30, Chamberlain and Hitler met in Munich and in the name of preserving peace divided up poor Czechoslovakia, giving the German-speaking parts to greater Germany and other parts of Slovakia to Hungary.

The frontier with Hungary fell exactly on our estate, which though leased by us, was the property of the municipality of Rimavska Sobota. Half of the estate ended up in Czechoslovakia and half in Hungary, while Rimavska Sobota was entirely in Hungary. Clearly it was impossible for us to live on the frontier of two countries, especially with our acreage so reduced.

One day a Czech policeman came to me and confided, "Mrs. Beykovský, your husband should get away from here. He's known as a Czech patriot, and if a bullet arrives from a Hungarian neighbor and kills him, we don't want to be responsible."

Naturally we paid attention to him, and Viktor went to Prague to see how we could continue making a living. He had sold a good deal of the cattle and the horses. As soon as we saw the danger in living on the border I decided to send our valuables to the Dovalas in Klenovec. In a chest that would have been appropriate for a steamship voyage, I packed up my fine linen tablecloths and bedclothes, our cutlery and silver bowls, and the little jewelry I had inherited from my mother-in-law. The chest was then covered up and hidden in a wagon drawn by two horses, under the care of Kalafuska and the coachman. They had to make a three-hour trip passing through various villages that were in an enthusiastic uproar over the recent political events.

When Viktor had to leave I was left alone with the two children, so we decided that I too should go to Klenovec. We sent the rest of the cattle there too. Mrs. Dovalova found me a rented room in the village and helped me sell the rest of the cows. I don't remember how long I was there. Eventually I sold our furniture and sent many of our possessions to Olmutz, where I then went with the children.

Viktor was still in Prague and was working with a company that wanted to establish a sugar plantation in Guayaquil, Ecuador. As an agronomist it fell to him to buy all the appropriate machinery and equipment. When everything was bought and prepared, there came the 15th of March 1939, when Hitler occupied Czechoslovakia, and the project came to nothing.

Viktor had many connections in various ministries, and one day he phoned me in Olmütz and asked me, "Do you want to move to Ecuador?" I replied, "Even if I don't know where it is I will go with you wherever you want, even to the end of the Earth." And so we went to the end of the Earth, to Ecuador.

OUR LIFE BEGINS IN ECUADOR, 1939-1949

When we left in the month of July in 1939, we were not allowed to take with us anything of value, including jewelry, silver or gold, furs, carpets and so on. So we left everything with my mother. Viktor had prepared the necessary documents so that she would go with us too, but Mother refused. She was old and would be a burden, she said, since we young people had to contend with an unknown life in a foreign land. Not only did Viktor love her deeply, but she too loved him and our sons.

TOMY AND VIKTOR IN PRAGUE

From Prague we went to Antwerp by train, and there we met a group composed of a dozen Czech families who were embarking on the same ship as ourselves. It was called the "Aconcagua," and flew the Chilean flag. The group included people who are our friends to this day, such as Dr. Lederer. The trip was very uncomfortable for me. Viktor spent the seventeen days at sea learning Spanish from a book and wasn't seasick for even a moment. But I suffered greatly from seasickness.

The three-and-a-half year-old Tomy was friendly with the sailors and they made him a swing out of rope. Jirko roamed the whole ship and also went swimming in the pool. One day a woman (the mother of Otto Kohn) came to me out of breath and said, "For God's sake, Mrs. Beykovský, did you see Jirko climb from the second class to first class deck by the ladder on the outside of the ship?" We were out at sea, so it's a good thing I didn't see it!

On the seventeenth day we arrived at Guayaquil, Ecuador. Some gentlemen from Immigration received us and found us a place to stay at the Hotel Ritz. At that time it was a big hotel built entirely of wood. The walls didn't even reach to the ceiling, so you could hear everything that was happening in the next room. The men had to put on a suit and tie in order to enter the dining room. At night you could hear mice moving about, and in the morning you would find crumbs of bread. But the huge cockroaches feeding themselves was something new to me, and I never imagined how many thousands I would see in the following years.

We sent Jirko to a local school, and the first day he returned proudly telling me that he already knew how to say "pencil" and "notebook" in Spanish. On the third day after our arrival came Jirko's eighth birthday, and I went out to look for a present for him. After a full day's search in which I found nothing I finally bought him a "great present", a ball that hung from an elastic string.

The foreigners we met in Guayaquil counseled us to go to the mountains, firstly because the climate was much better and secondly because there were more possibilities that Viktor would find work. At that time there was still a lot of yellow fever and malaria on the coast. So we took the train to Ambato. But nobody had told us that the mountains were very cold, and since the trip took 12 hours and went through some very cold areas like the "Devil's Nose" at 4,000 meters in altitude, we found ourselves shivering at times. We of course were accustomed to August being the warmest time of the year, which was not the case in this part of the world.

In Ambato we stayed at the "Villa Hilda", run by a Czech couple named Divisek who had already been in Ecuador for some time. My first impression was of the hotel's garden where, as I wrote to my mother, "Imagine -here grows violets, roses and chrysanthemums, and all at the same time!" This was a surprise because in Europe these flowers bloom separately in spring, summer and autumn respectively. In the trees there were plums and ripe pears. In order not to spend too much money in the hotel we found two rooms in a house in the barrio (neighborhood) of Miraflores. As the floor was made of wood the place was full of fleas, I had to mop the floor beneath the beds each night with coal tar.

Meanwhile Viktor had to look for work in order to earn some money, since we had been limited in the amount we could bring with us. He visited many haciendas (large farms) and plantations where they needed administrators, sometimes riding for two days on horseback. But the possibilities were reduced by the problem of a school for Jirko. One day Viktor met two Austrian immigrants who had some money and were looking for an agronomist with whom they could lease a plantation in Pillaro, which was close to Ambato.

The roads were still very primitive, dangerous, winding and rarely passable for cars. On the one side were huge rocks and on the other were tremendous canyons overlooking rivers. A German who bought cattle for his slaughterhouse did this trip once and said afterwards that he'd never do it again, not even if he were paid a million sucres (the national currency). Nonetheless, we decided to move there.

There wasn't even a house for us to live in when we arrived, so we had to live in a room in a building that they'd just started to build but which was never finished. The village of Pillaro was at 3,000 meters altitude and behind it you could see forest-covered mountains in which it was said that bears lived. One day I bought a bearskin from an Indian, and I kept it for many years. This part of the country had huge orchards of apples and pears.

Two huge crates had been sent from Olmutz with our possessions, including four beds, a table with four steel chairs, a set of porcelain, glasses, crystal, feather pillows, sheets, and the sewing machine my father gave my mother when they were married in 1892. The shipment had still not arrived so we bought a kerosene stove, some essential utensils, and four beds. These latter were made of wood but instead of springs they had thick cords laced the length and breadth of the bed, on which we laid mattresses. Every night we had to set rat traps, and every night they caught rats. The only source of water was a trench half a meter wide in which I had to wash our clothes rolled up. Jirko had to go on foot to school in the village, and you can imagine what class of education he got. As there was no butcher shop we had to buy a flank of lamb or pork in order to have meat. Poor Viktor caught dysentery and the only thing he could eat was rice and leeks. The village had only one doctor and when you needed him, you had to look for him at the store where he spent his time drinking beer, and was most of the time drunk. The owner of the plantation didn't want to fix our quarters and there were problems with one of the partners, so eventually we had to return to Ambato. Meanwhile our crates had arrived, so we rented a small apartment. The greatest relief was to have our own beds again, and our accustomed kitchen utensils for cooking.

Viktor had brought from Olmutz a reference for a family named Kubes who had lived for ten years in Ecuador. It is worth describing them and their life. The government of Ecuador had advertised in Czechoslovakia for a veterinarian, the first in the country's history, and it was Dr. Vladimir Kubes who was chosen from among the applicants. He was a bachelor, and like every one who arrives in Ecuador for the first time, was fascinated by the natural beauty, the variety of geography and ways of life, the differences between groups such as the very rich in the cities and the poor Indians. After a while he returned to Moravia where his fiancé lived; they were married and he brought her back to Ecuador with him. She was a friend of one of my cousins in Olmutz.

Dr. Kubes had two brothers, Vilem and Florin, who were millers and very hard workers. Since in those times (1929) it was possible for people to acquire huge tracts of virgin land by simply clearing them, Dr. Kubes brought his two brothers to Ecuador. Of course, there were all sorts of circumstances that they never imagined they'd have to overcome. For example it took over ten hours by horseback from the nearest town to reach the sites they'd chosen, traveling through countryside that didn't yet have roads. But they began to work, cutting down trees and sawing planks to make their houses, sowing potatoes, sweet potatoes and corn. After clearing more land they planted sugarcane, and this was the beginning of the estate called "Moravia."

After some years, Vilem invited a childhood girlfriend who came from his hometown to share his life in Ecuador, and thus gained a wife. Vilem traveled to the port of Salinas to meet the boat, and they were married in Quito. It must have been a fantastic trip for her: first the boat trip followed by her arrival in a country so strange and primitive in all senses, then the twelve-hour train ride to Quito, another twelve hours to Banos (probably by bus), and finally who knows how many more hours by horseback to the estate.

In the meantime Vilem had built a house of wood taken from the forest and mounted on cement blocks one meter high so that the dampness of the ground wouldn't reach the house -but also to prevent animals and snakes from climbing into the house. His wife later told me much about those first years of her new life in Ecuador. Using wood, which they had, in abundance, she cooked in the most primitive way, putting iron bars over stones and placing her pots on them.

She became pregnant, but when the baby finally came she was alone in the house with some neighboring Indians and the child, a girl, died. They buried her behind the house where to this day the grave is marked with a little cross.

For her second pregnancy she was taken to Quito for proper medical attention, but to get from the estate to the nearest place that had buses she had to be carried by two Indians in a type of hammock. This time all went well and she had her first son Wily, who was already six when we first met the Kubes family. His younger brother Robert was four.

Viktor had sent a message to Vilem while returning from Pillaro to Ambato, saying that he hoped to meet him. They immediately became good friends, and were both happy to be speaking Czech once more.

The Ecuadorians have always been very good with foreigners. They tried with great patience to understand us, though at times it must have been difficult for them to believe that it was Spanish we were speaking. During the time we spent in Ambato, while Viktor went to visit the haciendas that were looking for administrators, I stayed with the children and had to go shopping armed with a dictionary. My sons learned Spanish much faster than I did, especially Jirko who was already going to school.

Other foreigners had advised us to go to Quito in hopes of finding a job or business. So we packed up and went there, staying at the Pension Neumann, whose owners were Americans, as were most of their guests. If I remember correctly we paid seven sucres per day per person, meals included.

Naturally we looked for an apartment and found one in a neighborhood called La Mariscal. The Social Security of Ecuador was the owner of these buildings, which consisted of two floors with four apartments on each floor. In the middle of each floor was a patio where you did your laundry and where you got together to chat with your neighbors (there were Germans and Czechs there) and tell of your adventures in this country, which was so different from Europe. As we couldn't pay a muchacha (a maid) to do our washing I had to learn to wash clothes in cold water, something I'd never done before. A German lady living in the floor above always admired the fine linen that I had, all embroidered beautifully. Czechoslovakia was famous for its linen factories, and for the perfection and quality of its products.

The Second World War had broken out, and letters arrived from Europe with less and less frequency until the day they ceased altogether. As always we put Jirko into nearby school as soon as possible, but since it was a state school the children were from poor families and were continually stealing his pencils and notebooks and whatever else they could take. At that time we didn't know that better schools existed such as private schools or those of the Jesuits and

Salesians, but I think that in any case we wouldn't have been able to pay for them.

Viktor still had no income. He'd made a contract with Mr. Kubes who was supposed to deliver wood to make parquet floors, which Viktor would sell. He had pre-sold a number and had the men ready to put them in, but we waited and waited for Mr. Kubes to deliver the wood. At that time Mrs. Kubes was pregnant again and came to Quito for the birth. I invited her to stay at our house a few days before and after that event, and so began a friendship that remains to this day.

We had put Tomy in a public kindergarten where there were other foreign children like Tomy Eisler and Eva Braun. They became friends, and that was how we got to know the Eislers, who were both Czechs and experts in chemical cleaning and dyeing. Mr. Eisler had a plan to go into chemical cleaning and asked if I'd like to work with them, going to the houses of wealthy people to sell the cleaning service. They began the business in a very primitive form. The clothes were put in a drum of gasoline and difficult stains were taken out with a special liquid. The latter was the job of Mrs. Eisler, while her husband ironed the clothes.

At first I collected all the clothes on foot and delivered it the same way. After a while they bought a small truck and hired a driver, which made my work much easier and allowed us to expand our clientele. Mr. Eisler became friends with his Ecuadorian lawyer, who lent him money to expand "Iris Cleaners". They bought an electric machine for ironing and a washer for the cleaning. Viktor recommended the service to some Ecuadorian families he'd met through the parquet business, and they became my clients. I loved the business and brought a lot of good and faithful customers, but I was working too hard. In the morning I had to get the children off to school, and then return after work to cook. We'd eat, I'd wash the dishes and then once more I was off to work. After two years of this I was so exhausted that I went to see a foreign doctor who ordered me to leave my job if I wanted to avoid risking serious illness.

The apartment where we were staying was too small and

primitive, so we looked for another. Someone recommended a house in the Floresta area. The owner was a Czech tinsmith who lived in part of the house. The area was very pretty, with a lot of pastureland and few houses around.

Jirko stayed in the same school and had to walk the length of Galicia Street to get there. I remember being called by someone to look at something: there was Jirko coming down the street on a donkey, but sitting backwards and holding onto the tail so as not to fall off. It was quite a picture. People were always telling me of his pranks, such as the following one. In those days the city had trolley buses and they all had in front a sort of wire container the width of the bus, which was where the passengers could put their wicker shopping baskets. At the final stop the conductors had to change the buses' electric cables from one main line to the other, and turn the bus around. I was told that Jirko had agreed to do the changing, in exchange for the conductors' letting him ride for free in the wire container in front. He never really did anything bad -his adventures were always mixed up with some job or other.

I don't remember why we had to leave that house, but we went to live on Valdivia Street on the second floor of a house whose owner lived on the first floor. He was a carpenter with I don't know how many children. He was always beating his wife and frequently the children as well. I often wanted to intervene when he hit his wife but the neighbors told me not to, saying that I had no right and that a man could do what he wanted with his own wife. At the time we moved in, their youngest child was learning to speak, and the wife told me one day that she'd asked Tomy to teach the child Czech, only to be told by Tomy, "No, we don't want you people to understand what we're saying!"

Viktor's business with Mr. Kubes was terrible. Mr. Kubes never delivered the wood for the parquet floors that Viktor after so much work had already sold to clients. As he had even collected cash advances for the work, the clients were very annoyed when the floors were never begun, and so the business that had seemed so promising came to nothing. So Viktor had to look for other sources of work. He worked with another foreigner who had a door and window factory, as well as a wood yard that I learned to administer. Thus we earned something, and I also used my spare time to knit sweaters that we sold to friends for their children. We never had enough money to live comfortably and without worries, and at that time our situation was truly serious.

Once again we had to look for a new house because the owner of the one we were in had sold it. So we moved to the neighborhood of El Ejido, close to the park of that name. This time the house was big enough, and we were able to sublet two rooms to other people so that the rent wasn't so expensive. At about this time, Jirko finished primary school and since he liked working with his hands we put him in a vocational school called the "Central Tecnica." He enjoyed mechanics, but the students and teachers were of such a low level and the school so far from our home that I despaired of knowing what to do with him. I had bought him a fine jigsaw and together we had made many brightly colored little animals and vehicles out of lightwood, which a doll maker friend sold for us. So I managed to keep Jirko occupied with this, and it was the only way to keep him in the house.

One day his father spoke to an American who did electrical installations, and asked him to give Jirko a job. This he did, but he returned to us a few days later saying, "I'm sorry but I can't work with your boy. He's so mischievous that he climbs into the electrical work I'm doing, and the other day when I had a job at the airport he went into a plane and started handling the controls. They told me not to bring him the next time I came."

So once again I had a problem on my hands. Fortunately someone had told me about the Don Bosco vocational school run by the Salesian order. I went to talk with the Father Director and told him that Jirko had not been brought up with any religion, that we were of Jewish origin but that Viktor and I were agnostics, and asked if he would accept the boy. The Father talked with me a long time, asking when and why we had come to Ecuador and many other details.

Finally he said he'd take Jirko on the condition that the boy would pray and go to Mass with the other students. Naturally I agreed.

The Salesians are unique educators, severe but able to handle any type of boy. Recently Jirko told me that he wasn't very happy at the Don Bosco School, but when he finished his five years of study there he told me, "1 believe those were the happiest five years of my life." Well, obviously he hadn't been alive a long time, but for me it was lovely to hear this, and I had the impression that he'd been content with that period.

LIFE ON THE HACIENDA (THE FARM), 1945-1949

The year 1945 came and with it the end of the war. Naturally it was a great relief for everyone in Europe, though we Czechs had no idea how our lives would develop. In Quito we had a lovely "Club Czechoslovensko" where we had meetings in which the political situation was discussed from all angles, though nobody imagined how things would eventually turn out. The club also served typical Czech food and occasionally held enjoyable fiestas (parties) with theatre and singing.

After the war finished, many Czechs spoke of returning home, and of joining the Czech Legion that had recently been formed. Others wanted to go back to gather up the possessions they'd left there. Everyone was full of hope. The new Czech government had got in touch with Viktor, offering to pay for his passage and that of his family and possessions if he would return to work as an agronomist. They offered to let him choose an estate in any part of the country, or to work in the Ministry of Agriculture.

After thinking hard about it Viktor decided that he would first try again to find a job as an agricultural administrator or something similar in Ecuador, and if nothing came up, then we would go back to Czechoslovakia, though he didn't much like the idea. His opinion was that the best estates would already have owners or would be in the hands of people who had stayed in or close to the country; he wasn't interested in working in non- productive mountainous areas, and even less in working in the government where you could never tell what kind of boss you'd have to put up with.

And finally, he said that the Russians were too close and seemed interested in taking over Czechoslovakia. What great foresight he had, for not long after Czechoslovakia was indeed in the hands of the Russians and the people had to suffer all the consequences of Communism.

Luckily Viktor found work as administrator of a hacienda near Cayambe, a village north of Quito. The owners were brothers-in-law whose wives had inherited the hacienda. One of them, Franciso Espinoza, was a fantastic man, human and wise. And yet he still had the custom of beating his Indian employees. One day Viktor was horrified when he had to be present while a foreman was given a number of lashes for disobedience.

Jirko stayed in the Don Bosco School in Quito and Tomy went each day to the school at Cayambe on the Railway tram. The life there was new, interesting and enjoyable for me. I was able to keep as many birds as I wanted, including a brood of Rhode Island hens and some fine ducks (eight females and male). Naturally, I had to bring them all up from the time they were very small. The ducks began to lay eggs after half a year, and since this particular breed of ducks didn't hatch their own eggs I had to take the eggs to hatch in an incubator in Quito at a cost of ten sucres per animal. At that time ten sucres was a lot of money. When we first arrived there was one field planted with cabbage and white onions. Each week the hacienda sent products like cheeses, butter, vegetables and other things to Quito.

It was customary for the Huasipungueros - the Indians who had a plot of land in the haciendas - to send their children to Quito where they worked in the houses of the owners. Normally they stayed for a while and then were changed for someone new, but if someone liked them then they might stay in service forever.

Viktor frequently had to go to Quito to talk with Don Francisco (known as Panchito). For me it was a new experience to visit these families in their beautiful Spanish-style houses, with the great patio in the center full of flowers and plants, and the big family rooms on the second floor. I enjoyed life on the hacienda very much, with my birds and vegetables. We also fattened pigs that we bought in a pretty village called Otavalo, feeding them with the excess whey from cheese making. I received five liters of milk every day and used it to make butter and cottage cheese for our selves. Sometimes I had so much that I could take it to Quito to sell it. We also made our own rye bread. Making the dough was hard work. You had to leave it overnight, mixing the wheat, yeast and water. The hardest part was rolling the dough, and the whole family took part in this. The following day the Indians would heat up the enormous oven that was used especially for bread. Large pieces of wood were put in to bum, and when only the ash was left it was pushed aside with a shovel and the bread was put in.

To do my shopping in Cayambe I had to ride four kilometers on horseback, with my basket in front of me. Since the hacienda had a lot of horses I was given a very gentle mare for my use. My riding days had begun long before in Rimavska Sobota where friends who had a cavalry stable taught me to ride, and I had taken advantage of every opportunity to do it. The training had included riding without holding onto the reins and other tricks. Once we were sure of ourselves in the saddle we went out of the stable and had a lovely time riding in the fields and meadows. This early training came in very handy in Ecuador - who would have thought at the time that it would be so useful in a country so far away?

One of my most unforgettable moments was accompanying a peasant to round up all the livestock in our pastures so that the owners could make a head count. They were all brought to a corral and the overseer brought them through a gate one by one for counting. Naturally one or two animals were missing, but excuses were never lacking: that an animal had died, or had had an accident, etc. But that was anticipated and no one got very excited over it. These roundups were always impressive for me as I went out comfortably mounted and could take in the beauty of the meadows around me. Returning in the evening before twilight was particularly unforgettable.

The 28th and 29th days of June were the days of Saint Peter and Saint Paul, and a time for celebration at the hacienda. The Indians made great quantities of a fermented corn drink called chicha for these fiestas. They would come into the patio of the hacienda house carrying gifts for the owner, including chickens and roosters tied to poles and carried by two Indians. Among the customs was the practice of tying up the overseer and administrator (in this case Viktor) with leather straps from which dangled bells, and they had to dance till the bells rang. But the chicha was the most important thing, so that everyone got drunk and danced with ever more enthusiasm. At the end the women had to carry home their men, who were so drunk they couldn't even stand up.

We stayed two and a half years in Cayambe, and I enjoyed it and my animals so much that the time went very rapidly. We finally were living a tranquil, unworried life without any great problems. Jirko was well looked after and advancing in his mechanical studies at the Don Bosco in Quito, while Tomy was happy with his little trips to the school in Cayambe.

After two years the owners decided to divide the hacienda among their older sons and let them each administer their part. This meant that once again we had to look for another job. By chance I met a German woman, whose history I have to describe in some detail. She was married and had a small daughter. Her husband was also a farmer but since the marriage didn't work well she found a job as governess for the seven children of Gustavo Mortensen and his wife. The Mortensens were related to some of the best-known families of Quito's high society, and were both religious and cultivated. They lived in a huge villa on the Avenida Colon, which at that time was the most elegant part of the city, full of old, chalets in the middle of huge gardens. Everything connected with this couple was refined -except the husband. He fell in love with the governess, and after they began to have relations he took her from the house and set her up in an apartment where he could visit her whenever he fancied. Neither Mrs. Mortensen nor her family, who were important people, was able to intervene in the matter. Eventually Mrs. Mortensen was left alone with her seven children in her huge house.

This relationship lasted for years, and Mr. Mortensen bought his lover jewels and gave her money so she could live comfortably. But little by little he began to ask *her* for money, and when she hadn't any left she began to sell her jewelry.

The governess was an immigrant and known to the whole Jewish community of Quito. So when one day I met her in the street she invited me to her house and told me about her life, how her lover didn't feel much for her any more and asked her for money, telling her stories about when and how he'd pay her back. Her husband had once been the administrator of the Mortensen's four haciendas but he had left that post and the haciendas were without an administrator. At that time we already knew we would have to leave Cayambe, so Viktor went to talk to Mortensen. They came to an agreement about Viktor's salary, a comfortable place to live and so on, so they signed a contract for Viktor to begin work on the 1st of July, 1949. In due course a big truck arrived at the Alegria hacienda in Cayambe to take our few possessions to the Guadelupe hacienda of the Mortensens.

It seems almost impossible for me to describe the new place to people who don't know Ecuador and its varied climates, geography and ways of life. The hacienda was in a valley surrounded by mountains, with pastures and cabins going up very high on the mountainside. The place was called Pelileo, in the province of Pastaza, which is also the name of one of the biggest rivers of the Eastern part of Ecuador. It is on the road from Quito to Ambato and Banos. The road from Banos to Pelileo is incredible, a narrow highway with the slopes of the mountains stretching upwards on one side and a drop ff of hundreds of meters down to the river on the other. There are also valleys with cattle ranches, many orchards, cane and vegetables up till the Pastaza River.

We made the trip from the Alegria to the Guadelupe *hacienda* in two parts. Not only were we carrying our few possessions as I mentioned: we also had all sorts of fowl (chickens, roosters, and my beloved ducks) and a number of purebred piglets that we raised in Alegria. The latter were a lovely coffee-pink color.

On our arrival at Guadelupe we found a pretty house with sufficient large rooms for us all, as well as kitchen, bathroom and a separate maid's room. There was also space for my birds and a little garden where I immediately planned to sow all kinds of vegetables.

It was a special pleasure for me to walk around the *hacienda*. The main home was, about 500 paces from our little house. We'd been told that it was very big because at times a number of large families would stay there -remember that the family of Mr. Mortensen by itself had seven children, quite apart from any guests they might bring with them. But that summer there were only three of the Mortensens' sons there, and they spent most of their time with their relatives in another *hacienda* on the other side of the Pastaza. Around the courtyard was the house, and a large building where they distilled alcohol from the sugar cane that grew over a large part of the hacienda pathway ran almost to the banks of the river, and there they had a large plantation of oranges and mandarins. It was a novelty and a marvel for me, and a pleasure for the eyes. They also had avocado trees which no one valued -the fruit fell everywhere and I picked them up with pleasure.

I had brought with me the maid from the other hacienda, and we soon had the household nicely arranged. Viktor had his work and I had my plans to raise the fowl and plant my garden. We were content and happy. Then came the 5th of August.

EARTHQUAKE! (AUGUST 1949)

It started out normally enough. That morning the children said to me that they'd been invited to spend the day with the Mortensen children in the *hacienda* across from ours, where they were doing the corn harvest. Viktor ate his lunch early because he had to take a large quantity of alcohol from the plantation to the liquor deposit in Pelileo. He left at noon with the plantation's driver at the wheel of the truck. I was left alone with the maid and her one year-old daughter.

At about 2 o'clock a strong tremor shook the whole region. "*Caramba,* how strong it was!" I said and went back into the house, which had just been cleaned. It was a sad sight. The clay pots I kept over the wardrobe had fallen and smashed on the floor, and the walls of all the rooms were cracked. The maid followed me saying, "Senora, it's better that we get out in case there's another tremor."

"You're right," I said. "I'm going to the *hacienda* to call my sons by telephone and see what's happened over there."

As I've said earlier, it was about 500 meters from our house to the main buildings. I was halfway there when an earthquake shook the ground so badly that I had to sit down. There was a terrible subterranean noise, and when I looked up all I could see were clouds of dust from the buildings, which had crumbled. After the few moments it took me to collect myself went back to where my house had been. The roof was on the ground, and there was nothing more to be seen.

The people from the *hacienda* were running around as though crazy, looking for their family members. No one knew what to do or where to go. I was confident that my husband was in Pelileo, but what concerned me was how my sons would get back from the other side of the river Pastaza. Some peons arrived telling us that the earthquake had taken out the bridges, and that upstream beyond Guadalupe the river had caught up so much earth, rocks and trees that the water had stopped flowing -incredible if you knew the Pastaza in all its size and force. At that moment I saw my husband arriving on foot, running at top speed although there was no road or path or trail. When he saw me he embraced me, crying from the emotion of finding me alive.

It turned out that when he had left me at noon the truck had broken down on the road, at a point that looked over the *hacienda.* The driver had got out to look for the problem while Viktor stayed in the truck, on the side next to the abyss that later he had to run across. The driver had still not found the problem with the engine when the earthquake struck. Since he was above the *hacienda* looking down at it Viktor had seen me walking around our house after the first tremor, and then had seen it with the roof caved in. Thinking I was in the house he lost his head and began to run to the house.

Another miracle -later on we found out that the reason the truck had stopped was that it was out of gas, and that was why he hadn't gone to Pelileo! Over there, the Estanco had caved in and everyone in the building had been killed.

" All right," I said," I'm going to try to go to the edge of the hacienda and see where my sons are." The people told me it was impossible to pass over the river, but I hadn't the calm to wait around and walked down to the river bank where I heard more shouts: "Senora, your sons are coming!" Jirko was 18 at the time and Tomy 13 and a half. They arrived shivering; Tomy hugged his beloved father and said only, "Tato, Tato (Daddy, Daddy)." Then he told me that Jirko had grabbed a horse, and with Tom had ridden bareback to the riverbank.

There was almost no water to be seen in the river, just mud and rocks and the trunks of trees. Jirko took Tomy's hand in his, holding on "like a pair of pliers" as Tomy said later, and pulled him across the river. I said to Jirko, "Son, all my life I'll never forget or stop thanking you for saving your brother." We were finally all together and I made a promise that, come what may, I would never complain -such was my happiness at having my loved ones safe and sound. I said, "We've had so much luck that from now on I'm never going to ask destiny for any more favors, just be grateful to stay alive in these next few years."

Now. What were we going to do, and where were we going to cook and sleep? We were all exhausted, and it was drizzling -and every few minutes the hills would move again. As night approached we were still without a roof, so the four of us got under a mandarin tree with dense foliage. The maid and her child came there as well. The leaves kept us dry but I don't think anyone could sleep. The earth continued to shake. We were like a herd of sheep seeking shelter close to each other, anxiously waiting dawn.

The next morning we could see the destruction around us. The terrified livestock had hidden itself in the enormous cane fields that surrounded the hacienda. The peons were sent to round them up and bring them in. My birds were also scattered allover the place, and our beloved cat Susi appeared with her two kittens. We had been so worried about her; she had been with us for nine years and had come with us first from Quito and then Cayambe. At the time of the quake she had disappeared and I had thought that she had perished in the debris of the house. But somehow she had found a place to save herself.

My little garden, which was a short way from the house, had a dense hedge of pines about a meter and a half high. Jirko used it to make us a shelter. First he salvaged matting, planks and tin sheets from the debris of the house. The two lines of pines met at a right angle -the first two walls of our "room". Jirko made another of planks and made a roof of the sheets of tin.

But what were we to eat, and what could we cook with? The peons had rounded up the livestock and tied them so they could be milked. At least there was milk for everyone. The pigs and birds had fled. In front of the patio corn had been planted and it was ready for harvest, having still not hardened. The people in the area lived principally on various types of corn, from white to purple, and in all states from tender to hard and mature. They began the day eating "morocho': a white corn or hominy which they ground on a grindstone, sifted and cooked in milk, sugar and cinnamon. Delicious!

Our sons began to explore the debris of our house to see what could be salvaged. From the kitchen, a few pots and a few things to eat -I don't remember exactly what. As a stove we made do with two stones and some iron bars to hold the pots over the fire, so now it was possible to cook. There were bits of wood everywhere for burning. We were told that the Red Cross had come to help us but since the road was destroyed they couldn't get in. Jirko was the first to go by horseback to see what had happened outside of our immediate area. Actually, he went principally to look for salt since we had run out of it. We had vegetables and fruit from the plantation, and the Indians brought us meat as well as potatoes, sweet potatoes and other things that they'd planted.

Since the hacienda was in a deep valley and Pelileo was on a hill, the Red Cross had set up some tents near to where the village <u>had been.</u> They distributed some food as well as some ridiculous clothes and shoes that had been donated by the people of Ecuador and other countries. I say ridiculous because they were beautiful things made of silk and other fine cloths that were of absolutely no use in a situation like that. They gave us aluminum plates and cutlery and some towels, totally insignificant in comparison with what people really needed.

After a few days some Indians began to make us a hut. It was something new for us, and very interesting to watch how they made it. First they set stakes in the ground in a tent shape meeting at the top, and between those they wove leaves of sugar cane, so densely that not a drop of water could get through. One opening was left as a door. I don't remember how we managed to lift off the beams and slabs of what had been our house's roofs, but little by little we were able to pull out our beds, sheets and clothes, which we then arranged in our new dwelling. The first "room" remained as a kitchen.

On the 22nd of August came Jirko's birthday, which we celebrated with a feast. We killed a chicken and I cooked it with vegetables on my improvised stove described earlier. Later I made a cream sauce for it, and the feast was ready.

At the beginning of September it was time once again for our sons to go to school in Quito. It was Jirko's last year at the Don Bosco. Tomy lived with a family we knew there. For months the only way out of the hacienda was on horseback. When I finally went to Quito a number of friends embraced me, almost crying with emotion because it have been said that I'd died in the earthquake, and although they had asked the Red Cross for news of me they had heard nothing for months.

Naturally Viktor thought of leaving the hacienda but Mr. Mortensen wasn't to be found. There was no money to pay the peons, or to pay the salary that was owed to us. We had to wait for eight months before we could leave. By that time they had made provisional repairs on the road as far as Banos, which was the worst section.

Finally the day came when we hired an open truck into which we stowed our few possessions. On top of it I put a cage with almost 100 of my birds, and behind that Viktor firmly tied down our last remaining keepsake, my pedal sewing machine. My father gave it to my mother when they were newlyweds, a Singer which was one of the first you could work with your feet -before that you had to keep the wheel moving with your hands. In the earthquake by some miracle the head of the machine had remained intact underneath a fallen beam, but the foot had been broken into pieces. Tomy and Jirko set to work looking for the pieces and found almost all of them. A mechanic in Ambato soldered them together, and so our beloved sewing machine was "cured." Since the machine was made of pure iron you can still see the soldering points to this day.

STARTING OVER AGAIN, 1949-1957

I found an appropriate place for us and my birds, in rural Quito called Chaupicruz, a little way to the North of the city. It was a little adobe house with a big piece of land. We settled in, and when people asked us what we planned to do next we simply replied, "Rest for a few months!" But I couldn't stand doing nothing and after thinking and thinking I finally decided to kill some birds and prepare them nicely as they do now in the supermarkets -packed in plastic, ready to put in the oven and on the table. Luckily by that time we had a girl staying with us whom we knew from before. She knew how to kill and clean birds and so helped me with this, while Viktor began to sell them to hoteliers and restaurant owners that we knew.

One day Viktor left to offer some birds to the Hotel Colon, which was at that time the best in Quito. The owner was a German immigrant, Hugo Deller, whom we had known for years. When he first came to Ecuador he'd leased a small hacienda near Quito. At that time foreigners were only allowed to dedicate themselves to agriculture -

that was the condition for entering Ecuador. It gave rise to a number of odd situations in which European doctors or lawyers had to become farmers. There were thousands of jokes about these unfortunates, like the one about a foreigner who complained to another how he'd had to take a cow to visit a stud bull, and that try as he might he "couldn't get the stupid cow to lie on her back." Another of these fabled immigrants wanted to lease a hacienda in order to raise turkeys, but unfortunately in German turkeys are called "puter" and this man thought the Spanish word would be more or less the same. So when he went to the owner of the farm and was asked what he planned to do with it, he replied with careful pronunciation that he wanted to keep "una cria de putas" (translation: a flock of whores!). The owner nearly fainted, and told the immigrant to go to hell.

The truth is that the distinguished doctors and lawyers made something of their haciendas. But after a while, when everyone had forgotten about the strict law or perhaps after a change of Government, they began to do other types of business. For example, Mr. Deller went to Quito where he rented a villa and started up the hotel with the name Colon. As he and his wife were both hard workers, she in the kitchen and he with the hotel proper, things went very well for them. After a short time they rented a larger villa, and that's where Viktor went to offer them our prepared chickens.

They bought quite a few of them, and after some time went by they asked Viktor what we were doing and if we wouldn't like to work with them.

It happened that since April Mr. Deller had rented the restaurant of the airport of Panagra (Pan American Grace Airline), and he offered us work there, as partners -he would put up the money and we the work. We would work it part-time which wasn't too hard since airplanes only arrived at Quito as late as 4 p.m., though the restaurant had to open at 6:30 in the morning. They put an old auto at our disposition, and every morning we left at 6 to buy freshly baked bread.

But luck wasn't with us for very long. After a few months (as we found out later) an American bachelor offered to run the airport restaurant more cheaply, and Mr. Deller had the gall to send us a letter asking us to tear up the contract and giving us three weeks to leave. I was on the point of breaking down, having worked with such enthusiasm in the belief that finally we were going to have a settled life. It seems that I was so affected by the news that it showed in my face. One day, the airport boss noted, who was a fine gentleman, asked us why I was feeling so badly. I told him about what Mr. Deller had done, and that I didn't know what to do since three weeks would not be enough to find new work, and that we had two sons still in school and that it cost a lot of money, and so on. He reached over and squeezed my hand, and said, "Mrs. Beykovský, I promise you that I'm going to look out for you folks, don't you worry."

A few days later he returned from a visit to Guayaquil, called us up and said, "I've taken note of how you work and I like the way you serve people. Don Viktor, would you like to take over the Guayaquil Airport on your own, as concessionaires?" We were very happy and grateful. But, what would it mean to our lives? We had to make new plans. Once more we had to pack everything and move to another place -and again we had very little money. At that time also came Jirko's graduation, and luckily we were still in Quito so I could go to the graduation ceremony. I was very moved, thinking about the five years with so many obstacles, but when I saw in his hands the Industrial Mechanic's Diploma I was happy. He said to me, "Mom, I think I will look back at these five years as the happiest of my life."

We had to give Panagra a guarantee of 25,OOO sucres. That was my main worry but when Viktor talked next to our friend Dr. Lederer, he offered to lend us the money, without interest and to be paid back when we could. So we rented an apartment in Guayaquil, and received the inventory of the airport from an old German who had had it for some years and was now tired.

The work wasn't as easy as in Quito because the service had to be day and night. One hour before the arrival of a plane at night, a bus would arrive with all the personnel including our waiter. An original was this man: after working the whole day he would arrive all dressed up in his suit for the night planes. It was said he used to do his sleeping in the bus. Outside of his work he had a wife and seven children at home -in all senses German Lopez (German was his first name) was UNTIRING. Everyone knew him, and he was like part of the airport inventory. He knew how to look after the peculiarities of each client with incredible delicacy, and was always in good humor while at work. If you asked him during his late shift to cook something he would do it as well as his normal work.

So that's how we began our new life. Behind the counter there was a little kitchen that we called the "cold kitchen." That's where we prepared breakfasts -thermoses of coffee, juice, sandwiches and cake - for the Colombian company Avianca, which had a flight out of Guayaquil each morning. From the beginning we found this new work fascinating with the constant change in people: those waiting for planes, those with just 45 minutes between stops, and all the other movement. During the first month Viktor and I shared the work so that I worked until 12 or one o'clock at night then rested in a little room that was like a storeroom behind the main kitchen, which was behind the cold kitchen.

At night we put two folding beds with mosquito nets. The latter were absolutely necessary because at that time the airport was still not air conditioned, and the mosquitoes came at night in intolerable quantities. And not only mosquitoes but also, scorpions, which were even more dangerous because their sting could cause complications like lockjaw.

Once, while was in downtown Guayaquil, he was stung by a scorpion. It happened in a store as Viktor brushed past a stack of newspapers. I rushed him to a pharmacy and asked for a remedy, only to be told by the employee: "Senora we don't have anything for the pain or consequences of scorpion bite, but what you should do is go to the nearest restaurant and have your husband drink as much rum or brandy as he can take." That's what we did, and it was the truth: the awful feeling in his tongue subsided quickly and all that was left was a purple bruise around the sting.

We enjoyed the work at the airport, not just the variety of people who came up to the counter but also the great pleasure of finally having something that made us some money. Tomy also was happy in the Colegio Arnericano, where we were happy to know that he was learning English. In his free time he came to us and sometimes helped to serve the customers, or just amused himself as we did with all the coming and going.

Once, while passing by the souvenir shop after the arrival of an international flight, Tomy was surprised to hear a couple speaking Czech. He went up to them and said, "We too speak Czech!" The husband, a very nice man, said," What's your name, young man?"

"Tomas Beykovský,"

" And where are your father and mother?"

"Over there behind the bar."

The couple came over to us and began a conversation in Czech with Viktor. Our surname seemed familiar to them, and it was finally established that they came from the same Bohemian hamlet as Viktor. What a coincidence!

But let me get back to Guayaquil. After a few months there I got a letter from Dora (my mother's sister) who was traveling with her husband to South America by ship. From Argentina they had to go to Chile, and they were going to try to make it to Guayaquil. With that energy that is typical of Dora, she managed to do it, leaving her husband on the ship in Chile, she flew to Guayaquil. And so it was that one night, or more accurately early one morning, there she was in front of me. We could only look at each other and hug each other, and I began to cry as I have rarely done in my whole life. It was so moving: we hadn't seen each other for14 years. They had left their home in Yugoslavia in 1939 for London with their two daughters, Lore who was 14 and Nina who was 10 at the time.

Dora had only a day and two nights to spend with us but they were very moving hours. When it came time to talk of Tomy's future Dora proposed to us, or rather asked Tomy if he would like to go to the Ecole Hoteliere {hotel school) in Lausanne, Switzerland. Dora's daughter Nina had just graduated from the school, and through Dora and her husband it might be possible to have Tomy accepted. Normally it was hard to get accepted since because the school was always full. We all agreed with the plan, and as soon as he finished high school Tomy left for Europe.

But let me tell more about Dora's visit. As I said, she had only a short time with us; the following morning she had to be in Libertad, a small port an hour-and-a-half away by bus from Guayaquil. The ship, called the Reina Del Paciflco (Queen of the Pacific), was too big to dock in Guayaquil. Dora and I left Guayaquil by bus in the afternoon and got a room at a little hotel on the banks of the ocean in order to see the arrival of the ship in the morning. But we didn't sleep, just talked and talked the whole night through. I told her about the first years in Ecuador, and my problems and worries before we ended up in Guayaquil. We were told that we had to be ready at 8 am to take a launch out to the huge ship. Being Europeans we were there on time, and had to wait for another passenger, a woman who was to embark like Dora on the Queen of the Pacific. On the horizon we saw the silhouette of the ship appear, a unique and moving sensation. But... the other passenger didn't show up; we sent someone to call her but her makeup and coiffure weren't yet perfect, and when she finally arrived we had lost an hour. When we finally went onboard ship we found Arthur, Dora's husband, in despair. And with reason because he'd had prepared a champagne breakfast for us, and now there was no time to eat it. What a tragedy! All because of that senora.

We took the elevator up to the Sternes' quarters. I'd never seen anything so luxurious in all my life. An embrace - and it was time to descend once again to the humble launch and return to my routine life again. The "interruption" had lasted less than two days, but it was unforgettable both for Tom and for me.

As we finally had a solid business and sales were rising every day, we were able to save money and to pay back Dr. Lederer quite quickly. Viktor was justly proud to be able to return the loan faster than expected. Soon we were able to hire someone to look after the night shift. Panagra let us use their bus, and since we were at the market every morning to buy fruit, vegetables, meat and all the other necessities, they picked us up there at 8 each morning, bringing us a few minutes later to the airport.

The first flight was Avianca as I mentioned before, so the first step in the daily routine was to load the plane with breakfast. At that time no four-engines planes used the airport; the largest had only two. Since the trip to Lima took four hours, the plane also had to be provided with lunches that consisted of shrimp or lobster cocktail, consommé, a cold dish with turkey white meat, ham, cheese and garnishes, and finally fruit salad!

Unfortunately the company eventually transferred the chief of the Quito airport, the simpatico Mr. Bouvier. He was the man who'd brought us to Guayaquil and was our great protector. His replacement, Mr. Roth, was not simpatico, and was hated by everyone because of his way of treating people. I believe that he liked no one. Severity was his motto, and he liked to control everything. Only Viktor with his gift of knowing how to handle anybody, even the strangest or nastiest of personalities, managed to maintain peaceful relations with Mr. Roth. And so time passed.

Then one day came the grand sensation: a Panagra four-engine airplane on its test-flight. Mr. Roth said with his customary sarcasm, "This is the plane that will sink Viktor's business!" Why? Because these new planes made the trip to Lima in one-and-a-half hours and didn't need to take on lunch at Guayaquil {they carried it from Miami and took on more food once they reached Lima). Well, it was true that we lost the lunch business for these flights, but we weren't dismayed. The big planes brought more passengers, and when one of them was delayed for a few hours with mechanical trouble the passengers got off and came to us for food and drink. We met people from all over the world in this way, and it was both interesting and fun.

Luckily we had been able to buy air conditioning by this time for our apartment. I had to get used to the noise, but since Viktor's hearing wasn't good it never bothered him. And the machine stayed with us the twenty- five years we spent in Guayaquil.

In 1955 Tomy graduated high school and he was chosen to give the farewell address on behalf of the boys in his class. The following is his speech:

"Everything that came from my heart at that moment is little in comparison with what I really felt. I wish this occasion would never end: now that the time to leave has come, I realize how much I loved my classroom, the happy times that I spent here, golden times that will never return. I speak for all my comrades who I am sure will feel the same way: there were times when there were difficulties, small problems that because of our age and our youthful spirits, still clean of the hardships of real life, seemed like great abysses that we could never overcome. But here we are dear friends, some with a bit more luck than others, but all having arrived at the culmination of this student stage of our lives.

TOMY'S GRADUATION

If we look some years behind us we see that when we finished our primary education, we said to ourselves that we had had some years of suffering; but here we are in secondary school and we see that we have entered into a more serious stage; we affirm our personalities in making ourselves responsible for our own actions.

It is now that we are going to confront life itself. It is now that we are going to show what we can do, and what we're worth. I don't want to discourage us by saying that now we're about to confront something unsolvable –No, not at all. I only wish to remind us that we leave behind the kindness of the teacher, the pastimes, and the mischief. All the dreams of tender illusion have gone.

So here we are, sad and happy at the same time. And in this contrast of feelings there is something our lips can't fully utter: that is the gratitude that we feel for our teachers, the love we feel for our school and the affection we feel for each other. Faced with the impossibility of repressing it, permit me to sum up in these brief words that which should be the motto of our existence: Onward, ever onward! And finally, I call for a strong hand of applause in honor of our parents and our teachers. Thanks to them, thanks to their constant efforts, we have been able to triumph and arrive at this important moment in our lives."

Nina, the daughter of my sister Dora, was to be married on the 3rd of April, so we thought about sending Tomy to London in time for this event. We wanted him to represent the Beykovský family, and this he did. When he embarked on the plane the three of us ,Viktor, Jirko and I, were left in a thoughtful mood, quiet and almost abandoned. It was the first time that one of us had left. It was Jirko who spoke first and put it beautifully, "The caballerito (young gentleman) has gone away." He left a great hole in our lives, and I think that Viktor suffered greatly not to have "Tomicku" (the Czech diminutive for Tomas), his "little friend" at his side. He kept till the end of his days all the letters that Tomy sent during the years away from home, and occasionally took them out to read them, as if a novel.

Dora's husband was a very bright man and a great businessman, but he was an intolerable despot with everyone except his wife. He had said to Tomy that his English wasn't very good and that the first thing he had to do was to go to a college to take and English class. This was good advice in any case. Since he was already registered for the hotel school in Lausanne he entered an English course in London. After that his uncle sent him to Cannes, the prettiest place on the French Riviera, to learn French so that he wouldn't arrive in the French-speaking part of Switzerland without a word of that language. Normally, only very rich people go there, but Tomy was in a special summer school course for two months.

We continued, content in our enjoyable work. Jirko had found work, but wasn't very happy with it. He changed jobs and worked at a money exchange but after a while that business went bankrupt.

Fortunately, just at that time Jirko received his permit to enter the United States. It was something he'd applied for nearly five years before, but he'd had to wait his turn in the quota of Czechs who had applied (later on when Tomy applied it was easier to get in). He got everything ready to go, and without any further plans but full of hope, he left Ecuador. We were left alone, but that's how life is and we said to ourselves, "So, now we'll begin to live again, and await letters from our sons."

THE EARLY YEARS OF THE "PENSION PAUKER", 1957-1960

Our life in Ecuador followed the old routine. Viktor and I were always working together at the airport. I don't remember how or when in the afternoon we did our shopping, but we managed never to close the bar. However, depending on the scheduled arrivals of airplanes during the night, I believe there were evenings without work to do. Viktor had bought a second- hand jeep, and this helped us to get around. At home we had a 17 year-old servant named Panchito. He too was an "original". He began a relationship with a girl as young as he was, and naturally they had a child very soon.

One day Panchito told me that his little boy had digestive troubles and to cure it they were giving him a tablespoon of milk of magnesia every day. "But Panchito," I told him," you shouldn't give such a treatment to a baby -it's too strong for such a small child." Unfortunately Pancho didn't listen and his child died. Soon after Pancho had another child, so the death of the first one didn't matter to him so much. I told him, "If you give the new one milk of magnesia, I am going to hit you!"

He lived with his young wife and children at his mother's house. When he had three children he threw out his wife, saying that she wasn't worth it -and his mother would look after his kids. One day two nuns arrived at my house and said to me," The Church is going to marry for free those couples that are already living together without God's benediction. Please tell your servants." I first told Pancho, who replied quickly and briefly, "It's too late!"

We had a fifteen-year old boy who helped with the heavy work in the kitchen. He was the hardest-working and most pleasant worker we had, but a known homosexual. One morning he didn't show up to work on time, which worried us because he'd never been late before. After a while his mother appeared, asking us for the loan of 50 sucres. The poor boy had been discovered with another homosexual in a park, and had been arrested by the police, who wanted the sum of 50 sucres to release him. What morality!

The local flights frequently brought us the same people, so with time we became friends with some of them. There were politicians, managers of factories and directors of institutions. This is how we came to know a Czech named Dr. Mastalir who was the director of all the Olivetti stores in Ecuador, which sold sewing machines, refrigerators and so on. He traveled constantly. One day he asked the following: "You know so many people; couldn't you recommend someone who would buy from us the Pension Pauker? My wife's sister bought it some time ago, but she is frequently sick and my wife has to help her out and look after the business. I am getting tired of being alone in my own house simply because my wife has to help her sister!"

"We'll see," we replied. And when we left work that night we decided it would be interesting to see the Pension, which was entirely unknown to us. Things had been changing at the airport; the runway had been lengthened and prepared for the arrival of larger, lighter and more powerful aircraft. Eventually the day came when they no longer required lunch from us, having stocked up in Lima and Miami. I had always enjoyed handling a lot of work, and since this was reduced I said to Viktor: "You know, I'm going to look for a little job somewhere. There's enough work here for one person, but I'm getting bored." And since this decision of mine came at the same time as the question of the Pension, one night we decided to go and have a look at it.

The Pension was in a part of the city where we'd never been to before. It was in a building of six stories, and occupied part of the first floor. We entered the badly lit dining room, and were the only customers. A girl offered us chicken or beef, I think, saying that's all there was. We ate something and when we asked about the owner we were told that she was ill and couldn't come out. So we left without seeing anything else other than the dining room. A few days later we called the sister by telephone and made a date to drop by and get more information. I don't remember with whom or how long we talked, but quite quickly we reached an agreement to buy the place. The price was 70,000 sucres.

The Pension occupied two of the three apartments of the first floor. I believe that at that time it only had six rooms to rent because the owner lived there with her son, and there was also the kitchen, dining room and storeroom taking up four rooms.

Between 1951, when we arrived in Guayaquil, and 1957 we had been able to save some money, so it wasn't too hard for us to pay for the Pension in cash. When we got together with the owner, whose name was Patricia Divisek, at the public notary to sign the contract of sale, she asked us (in Czech) if we'd brought the money! I assured her that indeed I had. Later Viktor and I had a gentle laugh about the worried expression with which she'd asked the question.

We'd agreed that I would stay with Patricia for fifteen days in the Pension to learn how she'd run the business. They had a cook, a cook's assistant and a chambermaid, and I don't remember who they had serving in the dining room. I was accustomed to shopping wholesale for the airport, in large quantities. The Pension had always bought small quantities, and not in the places where they could get the best prices. It wasn't necessary for them to work with me for fifteen days. After only a week I said, "Thank you, I can do this myself now." They were happy with that, and so was I. Naturally Viktor started up his beloved accounting, so detailed and correct, not so much out of necessity but because it was his hobby. At the Airport he hired a woman to help a little, which gave him some free time to come and give me a hand at the Pension.

Around the time we moved into the Pension ourselves it happened that the third apartment on our floor came free. We quickly acquired it, and thus made our business somewhat bigger. The kitchen was a small room; we left it as a scullery and put a big freezer there also. Then we converted the room in front of it into a lovely roomy kitchen with three ranges and two ovens. The chambermaid Rosita stayed with us for eight years, a loyal and honored employee. Even now as I write these lines in 1985, she is still there working at the Pension Pauker.

We never changed its name for the simple reason that there were many foreigners who knew it. We also had the advantage of knowing so many people from the airport years, and so the new business ran well from the beginning. Frankly, the whole thing fascinated me; from the first day I enjoyed the comings and goings of the clientele.

Jirko had been in the United States since 1957, working first in Miami as a waiter and I don't know what other jobs. Then he had the good idea of volunteering for the Air Force for four years. Things went well for him there. He learned a lot about mechanics and was well liked, and once was picked as best man of the month with his photo placed on the wan with those who'd won the other months. Since everything in the Air Force was free (food, uniform, etc.), Jirko was able to save money from his small salary and eventually bought a car.

He began to make trips from the Air base, which is near Everett in the state of Washington. We were pleased to hear that he had gone to visit his cousin Renate Wilson, the daughter of my sister Margit, who lived in Vancouver, Canada. She was married to a Scot and had three small sons who, to this day when they are grown up, have taken Jirko to their hearts. He became a great friend of Renate's.

Viktor and I were both anxious to get out of Guayaquil for a while after so many years and so much work; especially Viktor who'd had no vacation since our arrival in Ecuador. We had paid off all our debts and had even managed to save some money. Through a hotelier's newspaper we advertised for a person or couple to take over the business, and eventually got an offer from a couple that had worked in Chilean hotels. They were of German origin, both tall and blond and raised as Germans. The husband promised to take over the airport work and his wife, Senora Daisy, to look after the Pension. They weren't very well liked, especially her. Our employees in both businesses were accustomed to strict but friendly and just treatment from us, and this woman never looked for the good side of people. But we never doubted their honesty until our return from abroad.

Before we left we had been proud to win a large contract to provide meals for a Dutch company that was participating in the construction of a new port for Guayaquil. It was a huge project and assured us work for a long period. Every day the company sent coolers to the Pension, which we filled with the requested order of food. Senora Daisy had to send invoices every fifteen days and, perhaps thinking she was doing us a favor, had invoiced more meals than were actually sent. What a disgrace, something that we would never have done. And inevitably the company discovered the fraud and soon took away this lovely contract.

Luckily we didn't know this till our return, and so were able to enjoy our vacation. We had been to see Jirko! He was by this time in his second year with the Air Force at the base in Everett. We were able thus to see a beautiful part of the United States, the State of Washington is truly correct in calling itself "The Evergreen State." It was mostly forest that we passed in our enjoyable trips with Jirko in his car. It was a bit old, and Viktor helped him get a newer one.

One day we traveled to Vancouver to visit Renate and her family. Her little boys were probably eight, six and four at the time. I remember also a beautiful trip to a lake surrounded by forested mountains. Huge trees trunks were brought down to the lake where they were made into rafts and floated from there down a river that flowed out of the lake. We stayed overnight in a pretty hotel, and it was there I had a quiet conversation with Jirko in which he confided,

"I think this Christmas I may go to New York and marry Ligia." I replied, "Well done. I like this girl because she's a hard worker, and I think she'll make a good wife." As it happened, things turned out differently.

Returning to Guayaquil with so many pleasant impressions we set ourselves again to hard work. We weren't very happy with the way the Senora Daisy and her husband had run the business, and they also were uncomfortable with Guayaquil and the ambience of the Pension. So we agreed to undo the contract with them, and they left. We were happy to be by ourselves again.

It was in 1957, the year we bought the Pension that Tomy returned from the hotel school in Switzerland. He asked around in various places, but we had always doubted that there would be work available in Ecuador where hotel owners weren't used to paying the salary of someone so well qualified.

Although we enjoyed having Tomy with us, we had to agree to his desire to go to the United States to find work. He wrote us saying that wherever he had looked for work, the hotel owners always asked if he had done his military service, and that he had always told them the truth, no, he hadn't. And they always replied that they would call him eventually. The truth was that the hoteliers didn't want to hire a young man who had not yet done his military service. There was always the chance that he would be called up after they had invested time in training him, thus taking away a valuable employee. So Tomy decided to enlist voluntarily in the Air Force, which meant that for four years he'd be a military man. We worried about this, since four years seemed to us a long time, but we had to agree since his decisions were always rational ones.

And what a surprise when he wrote to say that he was to be sent for two years to Japan! So far away! This was in 1959. Viktor had always enjoyed Tomy's letters from Europe, and now came interesting ones from Japan. For example he told us that whenever there were fights or arguments between Americans and Japanese, the American always got the blame. The two years passed rapidly, and on his return from Japan Tomy took his vacation with us at home. What a nice time we spent together.

The Pension grew little by little. I believe that Viktor left the Airport in 1958, since the Pension was sufficient work for both of us. As apartments came free on the second floor we took them over, as we had done with all the apartments on the first floor. Each had five rooms and a bathroom, and we modernized them with hot water tanks. In some we also put air conditioning.

Our kitchen had made a name for itself in Guayaquil and among certain businesses, for instance with Germans in a shipping firm, and Czechs in the chemical trade, and machinery salesmen and so on. I had never liked to cook, but I was able to teach our cook to prepare any type of foreign meal. She was a black woman with a great will to learn and a fine palate, which seemed to me the most important thing. So for German clients we made Kartoffelpuffer mit Apfelpuree - it like a tortilla, with dough made from raw sliced potatoes mixed with flour and egg, all served in a puree with apples. The young men were touched to be able to eat their homeland's food, and ate till they couldn't eat any more. For the Czechs we naturally made Knedliky (dumplings) with roast pork and sauerkraut. And so it went, giving us the great pleasure of serving different people their favorite cuisine and making everyone happy.

Managing Maria the cook wasn't easy. She had a rather special personality but she was very loyal and hardworking. Sometimes she fought with other employees, and Viktor was the only person who could make peace between them. At one point we wondered whether we would have to fire her for her belligerence, but Viktor spoke with her in a way that she promised to improve her attitude and thus we had peace for a time.

Twice a week we went to the central market. Eventually we had it so organized that we got all our shopping done in an hour, from 7 till 8 am. I bought all sorts of vegetables and fruits on the lower floor, while up above Viktor bought meat and fish.

GRANDCHILDREN AND TRAVELS, 1960-1962

At Christmas of 1961 I received a telegram from Jirko: "INTEND TO MARRY DECEMBER 28TH." I replied, "THOUGH I DON'T KNOW WHOM, CONGRATULATIONS." What else could I say? He was married by an Air Force chaplain at the base. His wife Barbara was from Everett, and had a two-year-old son named Steven. We were sent a photo of the wedding; for more we would have to wait until we could meet them personally.

The Pension and our usual routine kept us so busy that the days and months flew by. The Pension Pauker had become better and better known, and so many different people came from so many different places that life was never boring for us. Viktor kept busy with his beloved accounting, and his beloved game of Bridge. He was even asked to teach Bridge classes.

I almost forgot, in March of 1960, my sister Dora invited me to go to visit her in London and then to travel with her to Israel. But first we went to Vienna to visit our beloved cousin, Marianne Blaschke. Hers is a story in itself. She had spent a lot of time with us in Olmutz, living with us in our house like a fifth sister. When we were all yet unmarried an extraordinary harmony reigned in the house. We laughed all the time, and played jokes.

But eventually she, Dora and Margit were of an age to have suitors. Marianne went to work for Dr. Rudi Bacher, a radiologist who accepted her in his clinic despite her youth. He was one of the first radiologists. At that time they knew of the great potential of X-rays but not the dangers. The rays were used directly on the human body, and many people suffered terrible burns as a result. Soon the doctors used aprons and gloves of heavy rubber. But poor Dr. Bacher had been one of the first in the field, and when the dangers were finally known it was too late, the damage had already been done to him. His fingertips were already burned and being consumed by a type of cancer. Operations were necessary to cut off the infected areas.

I believe that he was over forty and Marianne hardly twenty when they fell in love. It didn't matter to her that he was ill. I remember she told me that once he asked her gravely if she really wanted to marry him, knowing that he possibly hadn't many years to live because the cancer had extended itself and there was no telling in what part of his body it would appear next. They couldn't have children because the X-rays had destroyed his fertility. But they were in love and none of this mattered to the young Marianne or to the mature Rudi Bacher. They married and had a happy life for two years. All of this was in Olmutz while my Mother and I were there, and we shared those years with them.

Years after the death of Dr. Bacher, Marianne went to work as a nurse in a sanatorium near Vienna. There she met a young doctor who fell in love with her, and after a time they married and opened a surgery in Vienna. There once again she worked as a faithful assistant. They had a son who was born, like Jirko, in 1931, and lived a life of much harmony and understanding.

When the year 1938 arrived, the Nazis occupied Austria. As Dr. Blaschke was an "Aryan" and Marianne was Jewish, they had a big problem. Only because the doctor had a brother who was a Nazi were they able to avoid Marianne's sent to a concentration camp. But she had to work in a factory each day. Occasionally the Nazis came to the house for some reason, and the girl who had looked after Marianne's son Ernst since he was born, took the strangest and most drastic precautions. Once she tied the little boy to a stout rope and lowered him down from the bathroom to a hidden patio. Another time she gave him some sandwiches and sent him to hide in the famous Domo of Vienna, down among the mausoleums of kings and famous people.

Ernst was very intelligent and a good student. When the War was over and he had finished secondary school, he left for Canada. He didn't want to remain in his homeland, which had made his family suffer so much. He continued his studies, and when he had finished and was earning his own money he returned to Vienna to be marry Friedl, his sweetheart from secondary school and take her back to

Canada. They now have two adult daughters and live happily in Canada.

But let us return to 1960 and my trip with Dora to Israel. The latter is the most interesting country I have visited in my life. My sister Ilona had lived there with her husband, son and daughter since 1939. They'd had the luck to leave Czechoslovakia on the day that the Germans occupied it, the first of March 1939. They went by train to Yugoslavia I think, and from there by boat across the Adriatic Sea to Palestine.

Ilona's husband was Dr. Kastor Kohner, who had worked all his life as a Zionist and received a certificate of honor when he entered Palestine. The son Imi was 15 and the daughter Lea 17 when they left Czechoslovakia. Kastor continued to work as a doctor in Israel, and the family lived in Haifa when I arrived with the Sternes in 1960. Imi by that time had married and was living in the kibbutz that he founded with other young people soon after his arrival in Palestine. We stayed a few days in Haifa where Dr. Kohner showed us the most interesting parts of the city, then we went to Jerusalem and finally to Imi's Kibbutz Amiad.

This was the most interesting for me. I stayed with Dora in a little house whose occupants were on vacation. The kibbutz had houses for the parents who were too old to work any more, and one or another of them was always away on vacation somewhere, so their houses were used as guesthouses. They had two rooms, a small kitchen and bathroom, and under the same roof a small area outside where the old people could sit and enjoy the tranquility. Young couples had their own rooms in other houses. They didn't need much room because at that time (not any more, I hear) all the children of similar age were lodged together in separate houses, watched over day and night by a nurse. There was a house for infants, even young ones of only a few months. When they began to crawl and walk they were transferred to another house for small children, where they stayed until two or three years, I believe. And so on in other houses, as they got older.

At that time Imi and his wife still had young children, two girls (later on came two boys). The girls could be with their parents certain hours of the day before returning to the children's house. At their parents house, they had some toys and some clothes of their own, but normally they wore clothes belonging to the kibbutz as a whole, which stayed in the house where they spent their day. Their mothers brought them back to the children's house, watched them wash themselves and clean their teeth and put on their pajamas, give them a kiss, and left them for the night.

The organization was impressive. At breakfast we went to the dining room and were struck by the variety of food they served, eggs of every type, coffee, tea or cocoa, bread in quantity, and I don't know what else. Imi's wife worked in the kitchen at that time, which had modem equipment like big electric ovens and huge soup pots. They also showed us their herd of beautiful milk cows, which were milked by electric machines and the milk taken to town for sale in huge tanks.

It was all so new and interesting for me, and it is difficult now to describe the marvels we met there. But I have a little story I still have to tell. Dora and I went to Amiad by ourselves; her husband was as usual very wrapped in worrying about her, and told me, "I'm holding you responsible. Don't go near any dangerous borders, I don't

Renate Wilson and Gaby, 1961

want anything to happen to my Dorli!" One day Imi took us in a car to visit some sights, and at one point he stopped and let us out, saying, "If you promise not to tell anyone, I inform you that we are now five meters from the Jordanian border." We both laughed along with Dora, who of course didn't tell Arthur what we had done.

After returning to London I flew home to Ecuador full of beautiful memories, and began again to work. Viktor hadn't had any problems in my absence: the Pension was now well known to us, the staff loyal and well trained, and the clientele assured. And so time passed. Guayaquil had never pleased me much because of its disagreeable climate. The humidity sometimes reached 95 percent, but I tolerated it because we were finally in a good business and I enjoyed our success. As we spent very little on ourselves we were able to save money. Viktor ran things well.

Tomy had always said that once his military service was finished he would go to Europe to look for a wife. While still in the United States he visited Boston, Los Angeles and San Francisco, looking for a place he would like to settle. San Francisco was his favorite. Then he returned to Guayaquil. At that time we had a German client who spoke perfect English and was well known to the American community. One day we asked him where Tomy might go to enjoy himself a little. He replied, "Oh, I am member of the Phoenix Club and today there's a fiesta at the club. Tell Tomy to go this evening and meet me there."

Tomy put on a tie and his most elegant clothes, and left for the club at around 10 o'clock. He returned in a half hour, saying that there was no one there. Viktor explained to him that fiestas in Guayaquil always began very late, so he shouldn't lose heart and had only to return at 11. Since Tomy always followed his father's advice, he went back to the club. And that was his destiny. He sat at the table of an engineer who was a friend of ours and worked for Esso at the airport. At some point in the conversation Tomy asked, "Who is the blonde girl at the table over there?"

"Come with me," said the engineer, "and I'll introduce you." It was as we say in German " Liebe auf den ersten Blick" (love at first sight). Kay had come to the fiesta with her parents. Her father, Allen Irwin, was a mechanical engineer with one of Guayaquil banana companies and looked after the airplanes the company used to go to the plantations around Guayaquil. The family was Scottish; in addition to Kay there was also her mother and her brother 14 year-old Alexander. Kay worked in a kindergarten for German children, although she didn't speak that language. But getting along with children isn't difficult and she enjoyed learning a few words of German.

Tomy and Kay became friends, and since we had our own car by that time Tomy occasionally asked his father if he could borrow it to "show a friend around." After a while he asked if he could bring her to the Pension to meet us. "With pleasure," we said. When she arrived we were surprised by how simpatico she was, for she said as she entered the house, "Buenos Dias, Tato, Buenos Dias Mamo (Good day Dad, Good Day Mom)." Tomy told us later that Kay had asked him how to address us, and that he'd replied with nothing more than, "Call them Mamo and Tato."

The friendship quickly became quite a serious thing. When Tomy went to Kay's father "to ask for her hand in marriage" (as they used to say one hundred years ago), the only thing Irwin asked was that Tomy find job before they married. So Tomy went to San Francisco, because that was the part of the United States that he liked best. Impatient to begin life with his beloved, he returned to Ecuador and told her father that he'd already got a job. And so they married.

It was the loveliest wedding I had ever seen. The ceremony was held in a beautifully decorated church that was used by lots of denominations. Our dear friend Mrs. Bush was a witness, as was a German client who had lived in the Pension for many years and was like a family member. At that time we also had some Japanese living in the Pension who had become true friends. We asked their chief, Mr.

Gaby and Dora
Lenk — 1957

Sano, to go with us to the church, which he did with great pleasure. It was the 14th of December 1963.

The bride was so beautiful that all the people were struck dumb when she entered the church with her father. Standing at Tomy's side we could see that his eyes were bright with emotion. The ceremony itself was short and beautiful, and afterwards we went to the Phoenix Club where we found a buffet and a musical ensemble. The first piece they played was a waltz, which Viktor danced with his lovely daughter-in-law, smiling lovingly at her as he twirled her around the floor. This was the most beautiful and moving moment of all for me: as I watched them I had the impression that Viktor had finally found a daughter.

After everyone had danced and enjoyed themselves greatly, we returned home while Tomy and his bride went for their bridal night at the Palace Hotel. The owner was a friend of ours, and put a bottle of champagne in their room. The next morning at about ten I got a phone call. A voice asked if we could fix a large and excellent breakfast for two. I recognized Tomy's voice but pretended that I hadn't and said, "Of course, sir, if you'll come immediately."

That very day they left for Mexico, where Tomy had been invited by a friend to spend his honeymoon. Later when they arrived in San Francisco, Tomy set to work to find a job, and quickly found one as sub-manager in a hotel close to the famous St. Francis Hotel, thanks to his diploma from the hotel school in Lausanne, I imagine.

After working there a year, his Mexican friend turned up. Tomy confided to his friend that it was his great dream to work at the St. Francis. As it happened, his friend recommended him and Tomy was able to realize his desire when the St. Francis hired him. I don't know how to describe the St. Francis, those who know it will understand the pride with which we were able to say that our son worked there. I don't remember exactly when Tomy wrote to tell us that Kay was pregnant and that their child was expected in November. How marvelous!

Our life in Guayaquil followed its usual routine. The Pension was by then so well known that we received many young men from Germany sent by well-known friends, some to work in the banana plantations, others in companies like Telenonna (telephones), and in automotive or pharmaceutical factories. Almost always, or perhaps I should say many of them began their life in Ecuador in the Pension Pauker. I still have the guest book where one can read the variety of people who stayed with us.

Some were scientists who came to study Ecuador's Indians. To do this they had to go deep into the country, living the same primitive life as the Indians. Among the guests were also some who went to Galapagos. I made friends with a Mrs. Wittmer who brought me her book describing her family's life there called, "The Robinson-woman of the Galapagos."

Since we had the Pension and its employees well organized, our life was calm but at times diverting. I filled the four large balconies with flowers, some of which grew so big that I had to transplant them to gasoline or oil drums. The quantity made for an entire garden of tropical plants, and it was a most agreeable pastime for me. I watered, transplanted, gave them new earth and admired each day how they grew. I had a high cactus with spines like sewing needles; one day I found that a colibri (humming bird) had made its nest among the needles. Later, after it had flown away and abandoned its nest, I took down the nest and have kept it till this day. It's a little bigger than a thimble, made artistically and gently like a little barrel.

In 1962 I passed a new milestone in my life, I became a grandmother. On the 24th of September we got a telegram: "BORN SON EDWARD VINCENT, JIRKO". I opened the telegram myself and joyfully ran to tell everyone: "I have a grandson!" When we received photos I realized that the boy was exactly like Jirko had been at that age, straight blond hair and brilliant blue eyes, strong and healthy.

Soon after, in November 1964, I had more joyful news: Kay and Tomy also had a son. His name was Andrew, and like his cousin he was blond and very healthy, and both remain so, almost thirty years later.

VIKTOR PASSES AWAY AND GUATEMALA
1962 - 1994

      In the years that followed, Viktor and I had the opportunity to meet our first grandchildren, both in Guayaquil and in visits to the United States. More grandchildren arrived with the passing years, but as my sister Dora has written in her own memoir, their stories and those of their parents are all "unfinished" and so I won't write about them here. Perhaps one day they will want to add those stories to mine, and to those written by others in the family who wish to add to the family history.

      I am glad that my dear husband had the chance to see his first grandchildren before he died. After much struggle, we finally lived a comfortable life running the Pension in Guayaquil. When he died August 17, 1975, one of his friends, the local priest, wrote a glowing eulogy about him in the parish magazine. The eulogy was headed with

Nina, Dora & Gaby
1962

91

NOV 1962 – VICTOR

JAN AND VICTOR   3/1970

these words: "The death of someone we love is more ours than his, for it is we who live it."

I finally moved in 1976 to Guatemala, where I continue to live close to Tomy and his family in Guatemala City. For many years I continued to travel to visit friends in Ecuador, and to visit Dora in her home in London and her second home in Lenk, Switzerland.

Viktor Beykovský died August 17, 1975, and is buried in Guayaquil Ecuador.

Gabriele Beykovský died January 5, 1994, and was cremated before Tom left Guatemala City, Guatemala and he brought the ashes with him and scattered them on "Little Mountain" near Mount Vernon, Washington.

CHAPTER 3

Jirko's Story

Born Juraj Harry Beykovský in 1931, I lived in Slovakia for seven years and eleven months on Sabatka Pusta, a farm near the town of Rimavska Sobota, which bordered Hungary.

For many summers, our family farm in Slovakia was a vacation haven to various cousins that came from as far as Zagreb, Bohemia and Moravia. It also included the children of migrant workers, including gypsies from Hungary, who crossed over the border to work on the farm. They arrived in carriages with the whole family, including their children and pets. On Sabbatical Pusta, as the farm was called, some pitched tents and some lived in dormitories provided by the farm, and others lived in their own carriages.

By the time I learned to talk, I understood German because my mother was born in Innsbruck, Tyrol and my father went to University in Germany to obtain his degree in Agronomy. I also understood Hungarian from the migrant workers, and of course I understood the local languages of Czech and Slovak. I attended first and second grade in Rimavska Sobota, the town near the farm.

My father, Victor Josef, farmed tobacco and sugar beats and my mother Gaby managed the household, and she personally toiled in her vegetable garden and raised chickens and geese. She worked to fatten her geese, as these birds rendered fat for cooking and baking, soft down feathers for bedding, and provided livers for her famous Pate de Foie Gras. Most importantly, some geese were distributed to the farm workers for the holy-day's 'goose'.

Each year, Gaby made sauerkraut and pickles which were stored on the floor of the attic. We had huge fluffy down bedspreads and pillows, and in the winter my mom would warm the bedspread against the ceramic wall of the fireplace and then wrap me up inside so I would fall asleep instantly.

When I was ready for the challenge, my parents gave me a wooden carriage pulled by a burro and I would entertain the children by offering them turns to ride inside plodding along the farm roads and trips to wade in the shallow river near by.

We had a dog named Lump who was always with us. She was a beautiful black Doberman Pinscher, sleek with a shiny pelt and very gentle with children. My father trained Lump in obedience and we considered her to be our guard dog and playmate.

When Tom was a baby, he would be placed outside to lie on the grass for fresh air and it was Lump's duty to guard him. We had many aggressive geese on the farm and it was Lump's job to protect us. Mom told me that Tom never fussed or cried when he was outside. She looked out of the window and noticed that when Tom started to fuss, Lump would put her paw on his chest and he would immediately settle down. The baby would turn his heard towards the dog and they both seemed to smile at each other, and Tom would go back to sleep.

Thanks to their foresight of the threat of Hitler, in early 1939 on the verge of the Nazi invasion, my father and brother went to

TOMY AND JIRKO IN ECUADOR

Prague to secure passports and a visa for Ecuador. The Nazis allowed our emigration, since father had a degree from a German University and the Ecuadorian government provided him and his family with an exit visa that secured our safety and destination. Ecuador needed farming experts.

Our family packed a few belongings, and rode the train for a couple of days to Antwerp in Belgium where the four of us boarded the ship called Aconcagua, en route for Ecuador. It was a Chilean passenger ship, and my mom said I learned to swim in a makeshift pool on top of the deck. My father said he purchased a Spanish self-learning language book that he avidly read and studied on the voyage.

LIFE IN ECUADOR 1939-1957

This section describes my arrival in Ecuador on August 18, 1939, until November 15, 1957, when I emigrated to the USA. As far as our dispersing, Tom moved away from home to join United States Air Force in 1960, and later in 1976 (after my father's death in 1975) my mother moved to join Tom and his family, who at the time lived in Guatemala.

Ecuador is located on the west coast of South America, and twelve miles north of the capital Quito, is bisected by the Equator (latitude 0). The country is bordered by Colombia on the north and Peru to the south. Before 1940, Ecuador neighbored Brazil, but subsequently it lost most of its jungle area land to Peru. The Galapagos Archipelago also belongs to Ecuador, and it is here where the explorer and scientist Charles Darwin developed his theory of evolution of the species. I've always regretted not to have visited Galapagos.

West of the Andes is the flat, subtropical area called "la costa", where bananas, citrus fruit and coffee are grown. This region is mostly wet, warm and humid. Ecuador's main port, Guayaquil, is situated here, and this is where Dad and Mom lived and managed the Airport Terminal Restaurant and the Pension Pauker, from 1951 until 1976, a year after my father's death from cancer. I lived with my parents in Guayaquil until my departure in 1957 for the United States.

In "la sierra" or "the mountains" is where most of the descendants of the Inca live. Centuries ago, Quito became the capital of the Inca country, and it continues so today, as well as being the largest city in Ecuador. From the beginning of the Spanish rule, Incas and Spaniards engaged in inter-racial marriages, and now Ecuador is a mixture of pure Indians who are descended from the Incas, Ecuadorians of Spanish descent, many Europeans, and combinations of all of these. Very few people in this area are of pure Asian or African descent, since most have intermarried. It is important to mention, too, that many areas in Ecuador have their own particular tribes of Indians, all of whom dress alike, maintain unique traditions and a slight variation in their Quechua language, distinguishing them from other tribes.

Many snow-capped mountains exist in Ecuador. Among these, the highest is Chimborazo, at 21,000 feet above sea level, and the Tungurahua and the Sangay, which are in a continual cycle of volcanic eruptions.

Quito is located 10,000 feet above sea level, and is where Tom and I went to school. The terrain is very irregular. The city itself is full of very old churches, and its people are engaged in a desperate quest to modernize. Although their "mañana" (tomorrow) attitude is still prevalent, they struggle to please, especially where tourists, a great source of income, are concerned.

East of the Andes is the semi tropical jungle known as "el oriente", with its sophisticated fauna and flora. There are several tribes of natives living in the jungle, but most of these now have contact with civilization. Airstrips built by oil exploration companies are used to travel out of the jungle and back as regularly as the more traditional river boats and canoes that are constructed from huge, hollowed out trees used with outboard motors. The native population trades in animal skins, rare birds and monkeys, bananas, coffee, cocoa, as well as tea leaves. Even the tribe known as the "headhunters " comes out on market day. Although they no longer decapitate their enemies, they do sell fake, but very real-looking, shrunken heads for a very good price, and try to pass them off as the genuine article.

Most natives in Ecuador speak dialects of Quechua, but Spanish is taught as the official language, and many also speak very good English as well. The various dialects of those people who live in the "costa", "sierra" and "oriente" are easily distinguishable. The prevalent religion is Catholicism. Centuries of Catholic influence have made it difficult for other religions to find converts, but there are many small groups belonging to other faiths.

The elected Liberal or Conservative governments change quite frequently, and are still regularly overthrown by the military as they were decades ago. Then the military stay in power for a while, and the people get tired of them, and the process starts all over again.

For me, Ecuador was a stepping stone between my childhood and my adult life. Looking back, I wish at times that I was never there, because life was difficult, but as my Mom said, we have to go forward, as we cannot rewind the film of our life. So, read on.

MOVING TO A NEW WORLD OF UNCERTAINTY

When my family departed by sea from Antwerp, the main port in Belgium, via second class passage from Europe, we arrived in Guayaquil aboard the Chilean flagged ship Aconcagua on August 18, 1939. We stayed at the Ritz Hotel. My most vivid memory is being served a plate of peeled very sweet oranges at the end of a fork.

Four days after arrival (my new name in Spanish was Jorge), I had my eighth birthday, and my mother set out to find toys in the local stores. After an extensive search in the city she returned empty-handed. She said, "I went to town to look for a toy store and found none. I wanted to get a toy as today is the 22nd, and is your eighth birthday." There were no toy stores in Guayaquil at that time.

Immediately after arrival, my father left Guayaquil for the capital of Ecuador Quito, where he started interviewing for the position of farm manager. He traveled to his first new job in the village of Pillaro, and days later we joined him. The farm was primitive and located near a town high in the mountains that had no sewers, no running water, and a dismal source of electricity. We were housed in a shack made of adobe with dirt floors. I can imagine my mother disgusted with these conditions as she was used to the luxuries of a modern home in Slovakia.

I walked to the village school carrying very little knowledge of the Spanish language. I was also something quite rare, the first blond haired "gringo" my schoolmates had ever seen. Soon after we arrived, the two pine boxes shipped as cargo from Czechoslovakia arrived with all of our luggage, and we then had the luxury of bedding, kitchenware and eating utensils.

My father summoned the foreman and obtained details of the farm's condition. Plowing is done with one oxen, seeding by hand, no tractors or thrashers as he had back home. The next day my father took me by the hand and led me to a plot where the foreman directed us to the land to be plowed. There was a single oxen pulling a plow, guided by a man in a red poncho on his feet wearing alpargatas which are sandals made from local agave, with a whip in one hand, he guided the animals with the other hand to work the land.

From 1940 to 1950, Gaby and Viktor worked at several farmsteads as administrators and learned that the skills they had acquired in schools in Czechoslovakia and Germany were very little help to them in their jobs in Ecuador.

The first home we rented had an indoor bathroom and running water and was located in North Quito, Zona Miraflores, Cally Galicia, was named Villa Nancy. We shared it with another Czech couple. Mary was the housewife and her husband, a huge black smith, whose business was to build metal countertop scales that used lead standards to weigh trade goods.

My parents, knew very little Spanish, except for what they had learned from books during the voyage, and they understood even less because most of what the farmhands spoke was Quechua, which is the local language in Ecuador, and not many understood Spanish. During this period between 1940-1950, very few children went to school. Other farms that Viktor managed were in Paute —"Hacienda

Guadalupe" —and in Tabacundo —"Hacienda La Alegria". The first farm produced citrus fruits and the second corn and wheat.

Meanwhile, at every farm, Gaby was allotted a small parcel of land to grow her beloved vegetables and, in the back yard, a fenced coop for her chickens, turkey and geese. Her managing skills with the poultry and egg production flourished in profits.

After working on several farms, Viktor pursued other enterprises, among them designing and selling parquet floors from exotic finished wood that had been harvested in the jungles of Ecuador. The Kubes brothers were to provide the wood cut at the farm, "Moravia". According to Gaby, the Kubes never delivered their product, and Viktor had to find another job. The Kubes farm was located near the town of Mera, at the foothills of the eastern Cordillera de Los Andes, and about four hours by car from Ambato. But their main products were distilled alcohol and raw brown sugar from their vast fields of sugarcane. They also produced inexpensive liquor by adding artificial flavoring and calling it "Rum Moravia". Bananas, cocoa, lemons and yucca were also grown there, but only for their own consumption.

In the beginning, before the tractor, all transportation within the farm was by horse-drawn wagons. The Kubes raised chickens, geese, and some cattle for meat and dairy products. They made their own butter, cottage cheese, and bread, and rendered their own fat. The smell of garlic was a permanent fixture in their kitchen, something that in my house was not allowed. There was plenty of fish from the streams and rivers, and occasionally meat from wild boar, or other jungle animals.

Once, for Christmas, I was invited to the Kubes and given an Ecuadorian silver coin as a present. Tio Florin, or Uncle Florin as he was called, stepped out of the house at dusk after the peons ate their supper, and hollered in Spanish "to cure", and all those farm workers who needed some basic first aid came for medicine. He provided them with Aspirin, mentholatum and other limited healing salves.

In its cities, Ecuador did not have any deli stores or indoor markets until many years later. It was impossible to purchase butter, vegetables or loaves of bread as one was accustomed to doing in Europe. Only Europeans knew how to make butter, and supplied it to other Europeans. Buns were sold instead of loaves of bread in stores and market plazas, and it wasn't until later, in the 1960's, that stores acquired the machinery to make and sell loaves.

My parents were shocked by the impurities in both table salt and sugar. In Ecuador, the shopping was done in "mercados", or public markets, in the town's church square, and the wares were spread on blankets or directly on the ground. Bargaining was a must, and the church squares are still used today, as they were decades ago, as central market places.

On Sundays and other religious holidays, the same squares were used for the town dances, parties, and religious processions and ceremonies. Meat hung on the same post where the animal was butchered hours before. Customers were given the slice of meat that was next to be cut, while swarms of flies hung around, and packs of dogs sniffed around the carcass, licking the drippings. No pre-cut or aged meat was available at that time.

Before eating all fruit and vegetables, we had to have them soaked in bacteria-killing chemicals. Although as children, we were forbidden to eat fruit before the cleansing process, but we ate it as soon as we bought it anyway. We ate other native prepared dishes that were sold in the markets and on the streets, as these foods were not available at home, and were a big temptation because of all the wonderful sights and aromas. It's a wonder we were never inflicted by any of the tropical diseases. Also, all of the vegetables and fruit were only available in their season. Tropical fruit came from the coast of Ecuador or from the jungle.

In those days, there were no refrigerators and to keep the flies away, we had a pantry container enveloped in wire mesh. Most fresh food was bought every second day. There was a market at a different church square in a different neighborhood each day of the week. Bunches of flowers were also abundant and available in season at the markets. On Saturdays, other markets usually sold furniture, clothes, and other wares, but these were at locations different from the food markets. As no "lady" would carry her own basket to a market, maids accompanied them to haul their purchases home.

GABY (MAMO)

All our friends and family called my mother Mamo and my father Tato. Gaby's first paid job was working for "Iris" the dry cleaning company in Quito. The owners, Mr. and Mrs. Eisler, at first provided her with a driver and an old pickup truck, and later an old van, and she went door-to-door seeking clothes that needed to be dry-cleaned. Most business was done this way, or by word of mouth. Years later, Iris opened a store in downtown Quito where customers brought and picked up their clothes, but after Mom stopped working there, other employees continued the home delivery service. Before the 1940's, Ecuador did not have this kind of service, and Gaby, cleverly, approached nuns in a convent and convinced them to have their habits cleaned.

Years later the Eisler's added a fabric dye factory. Tom Eisler had his hand permanently colored with traces of different color dyes. The Eisler family became very good friends with Gaby and Viktor. After their children moved away and Tom Eisler died, Gaby and Elsie Eisler continued to be good friends.

Another enterprise that Viktor started, was an operations and tourist director business. He leased buses and for a fee would take "gringos" on a day long tour to nearby spas. El Tingo and Alangasi were warm water springs and Machachi was a cold water spring, where the famous Ecuadorian mineral water "Agua Guitig" was bottled. The spas were in a valley about an hour from Quito. At Machachi they also had a swimming pool where the more courageous gringos could bathe in the very cold mineral spring water.

As a matter of fact, Gaby used the bottled mineral water from Machachi to boil her famous fist-sized Czech bread and flour dumplings, as eaten with meat and gravy. I remember her sour cream, dill, tomato and mustard gravies. At home, we ate beef brain, liver, kidney and tongue, among other meats.

Of course, many Ecuadorian dishes were intermingled with Czech dishes, including Yucca soup, cold fruit soup, papaya and pineapple, as well as purple corn soup for their Memorial Day holiday, and wonderful fried bananas with rice. Gaby also used the mineral water to cook fruit filled dumplings, which were walnut size balls topped with melted butter, powdered sugar and cinnamon. Gaby, who had hated to be in the kitchen since she was a young girl, did wonders cooking and baking many European dishes. Gaby herself had dreams of being a trapeze artist, far from the confines of the kitchen! Viktor, as a youngster, wanted to be a veterinarian doctor, but his father would have none of that. Instead, Viktor was required to be a farmer, following in the footsteps of his ancestors.

SUCH WERE THEIR DREAMS

In those days all travel was done by bus, available between cities and within the cities. Gaby traveled to deliver her poultry goods to her customers in Quito and she told the story about riding in the rear of the bus and being overcome by exhaust fumes that seeped through the old, cracked floor. She was so sensitive to the toxins and had to be taken to the hospital and given oxygen.

While in Quito, Viktor frequented the Czech Club, where he played bridge every spare moment he had. Viktor was very accomplished at bridge. In the meantime, Gaby visited her women friends at the Club. The other place where Gaby and Viktor spent their leisure time was at the Israeli Benevolent Club where, besides chatting and playing cards, everyone discussed business, and the war back home. The club also offered coffee, pastries and evening meals.

The profits from the club's sales and bazaar went for the Zionist cause, in Israel. Children were not banned from these clubs, but very few actually came, as most children were left at home with their respective nannies. I did not realize until many years later, well into my marriage, with the help of my wife Barbara, that I was actually a Jew. In my father's house, we never discussed this topic.

FROM POVERTY TO PROSPERITY

A Jew named Hugo Deller who was the owner of the Hotel Colon in Quito, offered a job to Viktor and Gaby, and, starting in 1950, they managed the restaurant at Quito International Airport, providing meals to passengers as well as airport and airline employees. Not until months into their new job did they have the luxury of financial savings, and they could at last employ a full-time maid. She was with us for many years in several homes and learned from Gaby some fine cooking and how to keep house.

Doctor Lederer was our family doctor, and Mrs. Lederer our dentist. Since they had lived in Ecuador longer, Viktor and Gaby always sought their advice. The Lederers loaned 25,000 sucres to Viktor and Gaby as a required guarantee to Panagra Airlines to purchase their restaurant business in Guayaquil in 1951. Dr. Lederer was a very kind man, with rimmed glasses, although he could only see through one eye. Dora and Arthur Sterne also provided loans to my parents, and they were repaid at the end.

I dreaded visiting the dentist's office where the work was done with a pedal-driven drill. The dental work was painful and was administered with the least amount of narcotic to save money. This is where, at age 13, I was fitted with a gold crown over my front tooth that broke while playing with the local kids. Someone tossed a rock that hit my tooth. The crown still holds well, even today.

The most profitable part of the business at the airport in Guayaquil was providing in-flight meals for passengers on airline flights. Also a source of great financial profit was purchasing bushels of live lobsters and selling them cooked and frozen to the passengers and crew for one American dollar apiece. A few years later, Panagra, which was a subsidiary of Pan Am, expanded with a new jet service, and my parents hired a third person to help manage the restaurant. Eventually fewer meals were required as airplanes became larger and flights were less frequent.

Viktor and Gaby purchased their first vehicle, a Land Rover, to use for marketing and their weekend outings. Gaby, the copilot, never obtained a driver's license of her own, so Viktor always drove. Later, they acquired a new Datsun.

In Guayaquil, one market was dedicated solely for all tropical fruits. By the 1950's, delicatessens became established and provided dairy products, sausage and other speciality products that my parents had been accustomed to in Europe.

German and Hungarian immigrants started meat and cheese processing factories, and managed outlet stores. Viktor kept scrupulous accounting of all phases of their business and Gaby managed the employees. They both worked very hard, day and night, to make this business profitable, and to their satisfaction it became a success both in which to bolster their egos and their savings.

In 1965, Gaby and Viktor purchased the boarding house, called "Pension Pauker" and managed this very profitably until Viktor's death as a result of cancer in 1975. Most clients came by word of mouth, were mostly foreign, and the rooms were full most of the time. They kept a visitors' registry that many customers signed with praise, and thank you notes in many languages. The Register is now in Tom's possession.

One year for Christmas, I gave them a special gift, a modern wall clock that chimed on the hour. Unfortunately, a customer that came to stay at the Pension had asked to borrow the daily newspaper to read while he waited for someone to join him for lunch. Later, when my mother came back to the waiting room, the man and the wall clock, wrapped in the newspaper, were gone.

My parents were very ethical about who stayed at the Pension. Several times a suspicious woman would arrive, and would ask to rent a room, and my parents would send an employee in to check and see whether she was a prostitute or not. Usually the local employees had very good sense about the intentions of other Ecuadorians.

In their blue Datsun, Viktor and Gaby traveled all over Ecuador and enjoyed their time away from the tiring heat of Guayaquil. Starting in 1965, they visited us kids almost yearly in places such as Mukilteo (in Washington state), El Centro and Salinas (in California), or wherever Tom and I were living at the time.

In 1969, Viktor and Gaby traveled to London where doctors discovered and removed a cancerous spot on Viktor's lung. My father said he learned to smoke in his early twenties to overcome the horrendous barn smell when he worked as an apprentice in Kocvar. Viktor loved Guayaquil and stayed there while Gaby, who abhorred the city and the weather, traveled to visit her sister Dora in London, and later in Lenk, Switzerland, from May to October of every year. At times, on the way to or from Europe, she visited with her children and grandchildren.

Early in 1975, Gaby and Viktor decided to travel to Miami to have a physical check up, and here they discovered that Viktor had an aggressive prostate cancer. Helpless, they returned to Guayaquil.

After Viktor's death on August 17, 1975, Gaby sold the business and moved in 1976 to live with Tom and his family in Guatemala. In later years, Gaby returned to Guayaquil frequently to visit Viktor's grave. When she was not able to travel anymore, on the anniversary of Viktor's death, she sent money to Rosita, who was their former employee at the Pension Pauker, to buy flowers for Viktor's grave. Tom's goal was to move our father's remains to lie next to my Moms in Guatemala City.

MY OWN STORY AND RECOLLECTIONS

We called Viktor and Gaby "Tato" and "Mamo" and eventually, many employees, friends and grandchildren used these names to lovingly address my parents. My recollections are that I spent more time at boarding schools, and on vacations at the Kubes farm in Mera, than at home with Tato and Mamo and Tom.

In later years, I was told that schools were nonexistent near the farms where my parents worked, so I needed to live away from home. I had always mistakenly believed that it was because I was an unmanageable child, and that's why I was sent away. In later years, too, my father confirmed that he had wished his children would never be sent to school away from home, as his parents did with him when he was ten years old. Viktor and his mother went to live in Prague so that he could attend school, away from his family home at the farm. Sadly, I was not able to stay in my home while attending school either.

I have brief memories about living in Ambato where, newly arrived, I spent time with the crew installing the water pipes in front of our house. Mom told me that I found a wooden box, filled it with tools and paraphernalia to polish shoes, and went about as shoe-shine-boy. In the early 1940's, when we lived in the Calle Galicia in Quito, I earned extra money by collecting horse and cow dung by the sack full and selling it to other gringos to fertilize their gardens.

In Quito, our home was on the top of the hill of Calle Galicia and all the streets were cobblestones. Many streets in the city, and the highways between the cities, were made of round rocks that were hand-laid, one by one. The workers, both men and women, used a bigger rock to pound the smaller rocks in place, and then sand was spread between the rocks, and lastly a steamroller came along and flattened the road. These round rocks came from the nearby riverbeds, were sorted by hand, loaded in gunnysacks and the local burros then hauled them up the hill. For fun, I rode the burros when the animals were not hauling cargo, sitting backwards facing the animal's rear.

I was driven to try different things. I was known in the entire neighborhood as being curious, and involved in everything and with everybody. I explored new territories with the local kids and spent most of my time out of the house. I am aware that I went to many schools, but I don't remember the places, the students or the teachers, except in a few instances. I was told I was a poor student and I wonder if it had anything to do with continually moving from school to school and from place to place.

Between 1940 and 1945, I attended schools in six different locations and I failed my first year of high school in Quito. During those years, I lived in four different cities and seven different homes. Information I have gathered from my parents lead me to believe I was always considered to be a child with disciplinary problems. I also wonder if being the only fair-skinned person among all the bronze and dark-skinned people had anything contributed to it. I was asked not to return to some of the schools and at others I barely passed the grades.

In Quito, we lived in the Calles Veintimilla, Galicia, El Inca, Avenida 9 de Octubre, Avenida Colon and many other streets with names I don't remember now. We lived on farms in Pillaro, Paute, Tabacundo, and in the cities of Ambato, Guayaquil and Quito.

In 1943, at the Sarmiento elementary school, I was called into the Principal's office and asked to close my eyes and draw a swastika. Now, I know they were testing to see if I was a Nazi or not. Fortunately, I was never able to replicate it and they decided I was not a Nazi. At one elementary class I remember excelling at typing skills. I went to both private and public schools. During two years prior to my high school, I boarded with a family in Quito while my parents farmed out of town. Later, I discovered that Tom, at another time, also boarded at this same house with the same family.

I joined a local boxing team and, at the time of the match, was told not to eat before the fight. I did not listen, and I ate before the fight, and vomited at the first punch from my adversary.

VOCATIONAL SCHOOL

From 1946 to 1950, I studied at the Don Bosco secondary and vocational school in Quito and graduated with five other students. Three of us graduated as machinists, and the two others as carpenters.

The Order of Salesians, Saint Don Bosco, originated in Italy, and managed this elementary and vocational all-boys school. Only vocational/high school students boarded during the nine months of the school year. Next door, the elementary school children went home every day after class, and this was a sad time for me, seeing all those children going home to their parents. We all slept together in a big dormitory on the third floor. Showers were on the main floor but there was no hot water all year round. It was lucky for us that we only showered once a week!

The options available for vocational studies were machine shop, tailor shop, print shop or carpentry shop. The first year started with 40 youngsters and finished with 6 graduates. The instructors were professionals in each field, brothers or priests of the order. The daily schedule, including Saturday, was as follows: mass early in the morning, followed by breakfast, recess, classes, lunch, recess, and vocational training in the shops in the afternoon, recess, supper and study time in the evening before our bedtime. On Sundays, we were allowed to sleep one hour longer, then we went to Mass, ate breakfast, and had a long recess that included visits from our family. I was banned many times from visiting with my Mom, which served as punishment for misbehaving.

My mom reminded me, until a few years before her death, of her disappointment at not seeing me during this period, especially after her long walk up the hill to the school. There were no telephones to warn my Mom that I was not permitted to visit her.

We stayed in the boarding school all the time, except for two or three hours on Sundays after lunch, when, under strict supervision, we went for walks, all of us in pairs in a row, to the park or maybe to a local soccer game or an outing to attend a special event. When walking in the park or other recreation areas, we would sneak and smoke cigarettes. Those of us who misbehaved were banned from these outings, as well as not being able to see our families or have company. I don't remember complaining about this situation. On very rare occasions, I was able to leave school with my mother, and only for a Sunday afternoon.

One of the highlights at the school was to belong to the "explorer troupe", similar to the Boy Scouts. Several times a year, at major festivals, we dressed in uniforms and marched and paraded in front of priests and lay dignitaries. I was included in the drum corps and later, as a bicyclist.

I was away from Don Bosco only for summer vacations. In September 1949, I returned to Don Bosco for my senior year, while Tom left for the boarding home in Quito where he went to a public school. Smoking was never permitted at Don Bosco but I managed to get into trouble continually by smoking behind walls, and would be caught because the priests could smell it on me.

While at Don Bosco, I decided that to be fully accepted as an equal, I needed to become a Catholic. I am sure the priests were delighted when I requested to be prepared for baptism. When I was baptized, the landlady where I boarded while I attended elementary school, Señorita Luisa de Morales, and the owner of the farm in Tabacundo, who was my parents' boss, Señor Francisco Espinosa, became my godmother and godfather. After leaving Don Bosco, I did not continue with religion except as a bystander at celebrations that were always very colorful. Translated from Spanish my baptismal record reads:

> "The undersigned priest of the Curia of San Blas by legal procedures certifies that in the parochial register years 1946-1948, page 58, register number 442, has the following entry: by the order of his Excellency the Reverend Monsignor Viktor M. Carrillo, Vicar General, the 24th of December of 1947, His excellency Apostolic Nuncio, solemnly baptized the youngster **Jorge Beykovský**, 16 years of age, son of Don Viktor Beykovský and Doña Gaby Kende Beykovský belonging to the parish of San Blas.
>
> > _This certificate is a true copy of the original._
> > _Signed Gustavo N. Naranjo L., San Blas, 20_
> > _February 1948."_

The ceremony was held in the chapel of the Apostolic Nuncio and godparents were Don Francisco Espinoza and Luisa de Morales.

Study and quiet time for us was on the second floor of Don Bosco, where we had a panoramic view out of the north windows, into the neighbors' home where some girls lived. This was always a delightful time. The only other time that we got to see females was on our Sunday outings. I graduated from high school on July 14, 1950, and the next year we moved from Quito to Guayaquil.

VACATIONS IN THE JUNGLE

I was invited to spend many summer vacations with the Kubes family at their farm in the jungle. This was relief from boredom in town and it was a real highlight in my life.

We spent most of the time barefoot, enjoying the wonderful warm weather, with a lot of rain, swimming in the warm river, catching snakes and beautiful butterflies and chewing on sugar cane.

I fondly remember eating and living among this very warm family. As kids, we always left the house early in the day and came back at dusk. If we did not get the chance to ride the horse-drawn coach, we walked all over the farm. We visited the sawmill, the distillery, and, at times, we walked with the farm workers to the fields to harvest sugar cane. We ate fresh homemade bread, goose and garlic spread on top of bread which was toasted on a grill on top of the wood stove.

Two lemon trees provided a continual supply of juice for thirsty kids and adults. This is where I learned about how they grow coffee, cacao and lemons on trees and bananas on palm trees. On very special occasions, Mr. Kubes would take a stick of dynamite, and after we'd hidden for safety, he'd light the stick and throw it in one of the deep pools of the river, and after it had detonated, we would all dive to gather the stunned fish. What every boy dreamed, happened to us. One of us always carried a machete for safety, and we used this tool to cut and clean the sugar cane to chew, and to cut roots that hung from very tall trees so that we could use them as swings. We did this like Tarzan from the movies.

My first vacation, while I was maybe 12 or 13 years old, started with Mr. Kubes picking me up in Quito and driving us most of the way in a pickup truck and, on the last leg of the journey, for about six hours, we rode on horseback. At that time the road to accommodate vehicles was not built all the way to the farm. The equipment for the two lumber mills, the distillery, the furniture and the building materials situated at the farm had been transported there on mule back.

The family was comprised of Tio Florin Kubes, the uncle; Vilem and Maria Kubes, the parents; and their three children Villy,

Roberto and Libor. I stopped visiting this family after high school.
Mrs. Kubes had difficulty with one of her pregnancies and she came to
Quito and stayed with us while convalescing. The other two children
were born in Ambato, a city closer to the farm than Quito. Both Mr.
and Mrs. Kubes were very heavy smokers. When in their kitchen or
living room, they would share a cigarette by Mr. Kubes breaking it in
half, lighting it and giving half to his wife. Eventually Mr. Kubes died
of emphysema from smoking and Mrs. Kubes died on the operating
table in Quito, due to a surgeon's error. They were both in the 70's.

During this time, I had a girlfriend named Viktoria who lived
in the city in Quito. She went to school during the day and I could
only see her in the evenings, however, the disadvantage was that I
lived by the airport and the buses stopped running at 8 pm. This meant
that I had to walk six miles home in the evenings after seeing her.
That was dedication.

Before attending Don Bosco school, in my spare time, an
enterprise that served me well while living in Quito, was to get the
discarded Bicycle playing cards from the Benevolent Jewish Club and
sell them on the streets. I had a shoebox full of cards neatly filed and I
went from store to store and on the streets selling individual cards or a
complete deck, to my neighbors. I was very entrepreneurial.

THE FARMS

Tabacundo. I was approximately 16 when my parents went to
work at Tabacundo, a farm located two hours north of Quito, located at
the foot of snow-peaked Mount Cayambe. Travel to the farm was by
bus or rail. A bus on rails stopped at a train station 100 yards from the
farmhouse. I remember riding a horse to town and getting to know
other youngsters, and one lad in particular that I invited for dinner.
Back then my father smoked cigarettes and he offered my friend one,
but not to me. My Mom noticed this and asked my father to also offer
me a cigarette. How times have changed now that we know about the
long term results of smoking. From here we moved to Paute.

Paute. I remember very vividly the August 5, 1949, earthquake while living at this farm. The owner had two farms and Tom and I were invited to spend the day on the other farm across the River Pastaza from where we lived. In the middle of lunch everything trembled and we all leaped out of the building. Once outside, we turned around, and saw the building collapse. We were lucky we weren't injured. The thick walls were unstable, made from formed pressed dirt and the roof was made of hay.

Outside everything around us was in a pile of rubble and Tom and I wanted to return home. We rode a horse as far as we could, then we walked and decided to take a shortcut by sliding down the river embankment and to walk cross the river.

Triggered by the earthquake, the river was now carrying mud and debris collected from the slides further upstream. Tom and I made a bundle out of our pants and with all my strength I tossed this package across the river. I grabbed Tom's hand and we waded across the river holding on to each other. On the road while walking towards the farm we spotted Gaby in Viktor's arms, she had been worrying about us. After her happy sighting, she stopped crying and welcomed us home. She thanked me, and she reminded me about this day all the time, for bringing Tom to her alive.

A section of road that led into town was destroyed, so a few days later I traveled on horseback for about an hour to the town of Pelileo, which was above the farm, to obtain donated essentials from the Red Cross. There was not a single home or building left standing in this town, and later, we learned that the town of Pelileo was the epicenter of the earthquake. The Red Cross gave us sea salt, matches, flour, sugar, and blankets. Obviously, our home was a pile of rubble, and, in the next few days and weeks, we uncovered our belongings from the wreckage that was once our home. The first few nights after the quake, we spent sleeping under a tangerine bush. The rumbling and after shocks continued day and night for a week, until "mother earth" finally stopped grumbling.

Quito is situated in the Andes and has the only international airport in the country where airplanes can't land at night. Airplanes don't fly into Quito at night because of the risk of the mountains so closely surrounding the city. The Boeing 767 is the largest airplane that lands at either Quito or Guayaquil.

Quito is the city where everyone is remarkably polite. They greet each other with embraces and dress properly for the weather, which is mostly cool. It hails, but it never snows. After people live in the city for a while, their cheeks become red and their lungs become very strong due to the high elevation of the city, and the shortage of oxygen. My parents and I loved this city because it was near the equator and the temperate climate allowed roses to bloom all year long.

1951 - MOVING 10,000 FEET IN QUITO TO SEA LEVEL IN GUAYAQUIL

Guayaquil is built along the river Guayas. The temperature is always warm, being in the subtropics. People in this city wear mostly white colored clothes and women wear very light, short-sleeved and very attractive outfits. The heat in Guayaquil is very intense; mosquitoes, flies and bugs abound, and the air smells of rot. Years ago, before air conditioning, we went to movie houses only in the evenings because it was cooler. In the hot season, I would sleep on the tile floor at home where it was the coolest place in the house.

Another favorite pastime was to go to the ocean beaches, about one hour from town, and spend the time swimming, sailing and having parties. Most of the time we suffered from intense sunburns. I recall the occasion that my Aunt Dora came to visit from London and she saw me with one of my sunburns. She very lovingly spread her face powder on my back on the reddest areas. From that time on I fondly remembered her by her soft hands and her kind nursing.

After moving to Guayaquil when I was 20 years old, we lived at 1522 Calle Boyacá and we stayed there until my parents purchased the Pension Pauker Hotel, and this then became our new home. In Guayaquil I worked in a machine shop but was soon fired for

JIRKO'S HIGH SCHOOL DIPLOMA

tampering with the time clock. Next, I held a successful position with the firm, "Casa de Cambio Tambaco". This business dealt in foreign currency exchange and real estate. I managed several accounts of homeowners who had used their properties as collateral for loans.

When I lived in Guayaquil, my friends and I smoked, drank at parties and we danced too. When together with the boys, we frequented nightclubs where we learned about sex. Looking back at all these adventures, I'm surprised I wasn't exposed to any venereal diseases.

I worked with a woman named Ligia Franco and she became my girlfriend for the next two years. Although we spent considerable time together away from the workplace, we never spent a night alone together. We were both over 21. She was required to be home every night, and on out of town trips, we had the company of her younger sister or brother as our chaperon. It continues to be the custom now in Ecuador for many women to wait until marriage before becoming sexually active.

On the recommendation of my father to his friend, who owned the electrical products company Sylvania, I was hired as a manager in an electrical store that had two other employees. In the end I was told that I had embezzled funds, which of course I did not, and I was fired. My assumption now is that the cashier, Laura did the embezzling.

Meanwhile, in 1952, I applied for a visa to immigrate to the United States, but because I was born in the Czechoslovak Republic, I had to wait my turn. I was on a list and many others applied before I did. Finally, in 1957 my visa was granted. Dorica Breyer, a cousin of my mom guaranteed my entry to the USA. In the same year,1957, my parents purchased the Pension Pauker in Guayaquil from Patricia Divisek for 70,000 sucres, and by now they had saved enough to pay cash.

A year, before immigrating to the United States, I worked with the National Cash Register Company as a sales representative, but I did not make any sales. I was sent to Bogota, Colombia, to a sales workshop to learn the skill. The manager, Richard Moss, who hired me, was a citizen of the United States who had lived in Japan before coming to Ecuador. He was married to a Japanese woman, and at that time he was the Japanese Consul in Guayaquil.

1957 TRAVELING DOCUMENT

Viktor was very well known for his skills at bridge playing, and very often played in a foursome with some of the best players in Ecuador. The last time I visited my parents in Guayaquil in March 1975, five months before my father's death, one Saturday afternoon I saw him playing bridge for the last time in his life.

JIRKO AND TOMY 1951

LOOKING BACK

In retrospect, my childhood life until 1950, before we moved to Guayaquil, was very chaotic and without a permanent home. I don't remember any adult that I could have used as a role model, and we moved from location to location so frequently, that regretfully I didn't make any long lasting friendships. We moved so often that I missed some basic schooling. It wasn't until sixth grade elementary that I attended a regular classroom school.

I was discouraged by my parents from having Ecuadorian friends, and I don't remember befriending any European children. According to them, Ecuadorians were not to be trusted. But it was difficult to make friends with other Europeans such as the other Czech, German and Hungarian families that lived in Quito, because they had busy lives of their own so I don't remember being involved with their children. My parents frequented the social clubs, but Tomy and I were seldom taken along.

In spite of this, I believe that what I learned and experienced during the first eight years of my life on the farm in Slovakia served as

JIRKO IN QUITO 1955

a solid foundation for keeping my sanity during all the future years of hardship we experienced in Ecuador.

Back in Slovakia, the loving care from my grandmother Amama, my parents, my relatives that came to visit on the farm, and "Gazda" the farm foreman who was my continual companion, baby sitter and friend, and lastly, my teacher Mr. Zajicek, all helped shape me to be the person I am now.

When Nina Hofman came to visit me in Washington State in 1988, she told me about one of her visits to Sabatka Puszta. She remembered entering the living room and being shocked to see me on my father's knees, being spanked. My mom recollected the reason. Before I was even four years old, she was knitting and was surprised by the silence in the room and, when she turned around, she saw that I was taking the battery-operated radio apart and its contents were strewn on the carpet. I suppose I was a naturally curious child.

GABY AND VIKTOR IN MORAVIA

Starting in kindergarten, my brother Tomy Beykovský and
Tomy Eisler became good friends but I have very little recollection of

interacting with Tom Eisler. I know that my brother graduated from
high school in Guayaquil and was asked to give the graduation speech.
My brother Tom traveled to London, England in April 1955, and was a
witness at Nina's wedding ceremony, when she married Max Hofman.
On this occasion Tom met Nina's parents and, later, was sent at their
expense to learn French on the French Riviera and also to Lausanne,
Switzerland, to the Ecole Hoteliere to learn hotel management.

I remember my father's sternness toward me and his lovingness
towards Gaby. He was always very friendly with strangers, but very
demanding of his employees and a disciplinarian with me. I don't
remember any conversations or positive interactions with him.

I looked up to him for his skills in playing the accordion and
the piano. When he was in University my father bought an accordion
and on weekends he frequented coffee shops with his friends where he
earned tips for playing for the patrons.

I had enormous respect for his skills at playing bridge. I used
to watch his beautiful hands, with their immaculate fingernails,
moving while he talked or while he held his playing cards, but he was

never to be disturbed when he was playing bridge. I was severely punished for not doing well in school and he never came to visit me while I was at Don Bosco school, and I was hurt he never invited or asked to work with him at any of his businesses at the airport.

BRIEF RETURNS AND ADIEU TO ECUADOR

Now I'll move forward in time. In 1963, when my son Edward was just starting to walk, my parents invited us to visit them in Guayaquil, and Barbara, Edward and I went to see them for a couple of weeks. Steve stayed with his grandmother. Over 10 years later, I flew to Guayaquil in March 1975, to see my father in bed, dying of cancer. This is the last time I saw him.

Mom had a woman companion to help her cope with this tragedy. My father died the following August, and was buried in the cemetery in Guayaquil, but I have never seen his grave. Rosita, one of my Mom's ex-employees from Pension Pauker, received $20 in the mail every year to buy flowers to put on Dad's grave. My brother Tom is planning to move his remains from Guayaquil to Guatemala City next to Mom's grave, and when he told me this I was very moved by the thought.

Although I never had any bad feelings about Ecuador, I hope writing this biography helps me to put to rest those tumultuous eighteen years there.

Gaby said many times that one cannot change the past by re-running our life as a film, but, looking back, I believe that given the opportunity, I could have done wonders. Although I look much as my father did in many ways, I believe I have many of my mother's qualities, except her pessimism. I love, just as she did, nature and the outdoors, walking, or digging in the earth growing flowers and vegetables. My dad and I liked all animals, but my Mom would have nothing to do with them. Both Mom and I loved to travel and I believe I am more tolerant of minorities than my mother, but neither one of us

JIRKO - USAF 1959

could ever stomach stepping on German soil. Both my father and I loved military music, and we were similarly punctilious in many of our tasks. I have my mother's poor teeth and gums, and my father and I share the affliction of prostate and cancer problems.

I wish I had known them both better. Our Jewish heritage was a liability in the past, but it is different for both Tom's and my children. Neither of our wives are Jewish, and, as a consequence, our children are not Jewish. I am always happy thinking that my children were born here in the U. S., and were not wanderers all over the world.

I returned to Quito to work with Western Geophysical, an oil explorations company, with Barbara and the kids from 1970 until 1972. I again visited Ecuador in 1993, with my second wife Helen for three weeks. We toured in a taxi and with a driver, north to Otavalo, south to Riobamba, east to Puyo in the jungle, and west to see the Colorado Indians. I was not comfortable taking Helen to Guayaquil because of the sad memories it held, and that's why I've never seen my Dad's grave in person.

It was hard to recognize many of the homes where we lived in the past. Some of the houses were not there anymore, some had been completely renovated, and others I could not find. The city has changed drastically. The evil ghosts and good memories are gone, and as I was leaving, I said goodbye to Ecuador for good. I don't ever intend on returning.

IMMIGRATING TO THE UNITED STATES
1957 TO 1962

NATURALIZATION CERTIFICATE

JIRKO'S NATURALIZATION CEREMONY

I had a lengthy wait to immigrate to the United States - five long years.

In 1952, with the Korean War at its peak, and a continual barrage of American war films being shown in Ecuador, with the United States always on the winning side and John Wayne always the hero, I fantasized that the US would be the ideal place for me to live. The best movies, the best products for sale in the stores in Ecuador were always from the US.

A visit to Quito by Richard Nixon in 1952, led me to apply for a visa to immigrate to this country. I did not know anything about Nixon, except that he was from the USA. So I applied and I'd forgotten all about it, until one day five years later, I received a notice in the mail, saying that if I complied with several mandates required by United States immigration, I would be accepted. I was very excited.

1960   PAINE FIELD

Later I learned that the reason for the delay to get the visa, is that I was born in Slovakia, and this country had a quota to limit the number of people who would be allowed to immigrate to US.

As a requirement, in Guayaquil I underwent a rigorous physical checkup, a police criminal investigation check and a I had to obtain a guarantee from a person living in the US, so I would not be a financial burden to the government when I arrived. The guarantor was a second cousin of my Mom's, Dorica Breyer, who lived in New York. Later, I discovered that the American government had also verified my identity in Czechoslovakia, at that time the Republic was under Soviet rule, so I was curious about how they could verify this.

When we left Czechoslovakia, children were included in our

USAF HONOR GUARD

parent's passport. After those passports expired, all four of us became stateless. Therefore, being neither a Czech nor an Ecuadorian citizen, instead of a passport, I was issued a traveling document called " Special Certificate #24", which was valid for a year from the date of issue in case I wanted to return to Ecuador. At that time, I had no intention of going back, not realizing that I would go back several times in the future. I wonder now why I never bothered to become an Ecuadorian citizen. I think, at the time, that the idea never really crossed my mind. We never talked about this in my home, and thinking back, I was never encouraged to do so. Eventually, only my mother became an Ecuadorian citizen.

On November 4th, 1957, I was granted a visa (#412) from the American Consul in Guayaquil, and with all my requirements satisfactory to the government of the United States, I flew on Pan American Airlines from Guayaquil to Miami on November 15, 1957.

In Miami, I rented a room at the home of Mrs. J.O. McKenzie, 500 SW 6th Street, and I lived there until my departure to Texas as an enlisted man with the Air Force. Mrs. McKenzie was an elderly woman who lived with her spinster daughter. We shared the living room and TV and we watched Lawrence Welk with his musical bubbles, every Sunday night.

In Miami, I earned money by working as a waiter, and for a short time I drove a Good Humor truck and sold ice cream. I delivered the Miami Herald, up to 450 newspapers, including Sundays, in a 1951, black, two-door Chevy, with a rambler seat. I bought it for $500 and resold for $200 when I left Miami for basic training in the Air Force. The paper delivery was in the evenings and my biggest challenge was attempting to collect money from the customers. Many subscribers left without paying, and some just did not have the money, or so they said.

During the day I would drive all over Miami Beach, Coral Gables and other areas to see the tourist wonders of Florida. The city was located right on the ocean, and the infrastructure was new, including the huge hotels with their private, cleanly-kept beaches, with the many bikinis filled with gorgeous bodies. At that time in 1951, I felt very safe walking the Miami streets and visiting many of its neighborhoods by car and bus. I was surprised to see neighborhoods populated mostly by African-Americans and in other areas mostly Latinos. I learned how to shop in a supermarket, watch movies and TV without Spanish sub-titles, and I learned how to speak English. In fact, I was surprised at how little English I had learned before this.

Tired of wondering about my future and with Korea and John Wayne still in the back of my mind, I applied to join the US Air Force and was recruited on August 11, 1958, for a four-year term. One of the requirements was that I had to go to the courthouse and swear on a "Declaration of Intention to Become a Citizen". While doing this, I also changed my name legally from Jorge (in Spanish) to George (in English). I was the oldest recruit in my group at Lackland Air Force Base boot camp near San Antonio, Texas.

In San Antonio, I was issued clothes, fed, and housed. I learned a lot of new things at a tremendous rate and I was especially happy to be in the company of many others who shared, common goals. I was proud to wear the uniform of an 'airman third class' rank (one stripe on the sleeve) and I looked pretty sharp. Since I was a machinist, a trade I had learned in Ecuador, I did not require any further training; I was therefore sent by commercial airline to Paine Field, in Everett, Washington State. I had applied to be sent overseas as an interpreter because of my excellent knowledge of Spanish, and also my limited German and Czech, but I was never accepted.

I worked at Paine Field from November 1958, exactly one year from my arrival in the USA, until June 1962, when I was Honorably Discharged four years later. During that time I accomplished some important things. I had a steady job five days a week, which very seldom required me to work weekends, and I obtained an E-4 rank as quickly as I could. I also became "Airman of the Month" for my good work and extensive civic knowledge and this resulted in several "3-day-passes", which meant I had leave of absence from the base with pay. But my most important accomplishment was becoming a citizen of the United States on September 11, 1961. My cousin Renate Wilson came from Canada to witness the ceremony.

I travelled many times during this period. I rode the bus to the big city, Seattle, and after meeting Renate and her family for the first time, I was their guest quite often in Vancouver, Canada. I flew free of charge on military airplanes several times, once to Quito, Ecuador, once to Reno, Nevada and once to an Air Force Base in Florida.

Later, with Mom and Dad I drove to Stevens Pass and Mount Baker ski lodge to experience the snow and the mountains, in my newly acquired 1955 blue and white Ford. Also, the three of us went to visit the Wilson's in Vancouver Canada.

Once I had the means of transportation, traveling in my spare time became my main recreation. I explored other mountain passes and other cities, as well as some of the beautiful local lakes and the shores of Puget Sound and the beaches of the Pacific Ocean, where I swam and fished. And for the first time, I went to drive-in movies. My address was Box 29, Paine Field Air Force Base, Everett Washington. Back then there were no zip codes. Mom and Dad purchased a Ford for me in 1960 and together we drove for days on this vacation, visiting much of Washington State and Vancouver, to visit our relatives the Wilson's.

I was privileged also to belong to the Paine Field Honor Guard, a group of selected airmen whose duty it was to represent the base and the Air Force during special parade occasions. My uniform included shiny black boots and white gloves.

And while I was at Paine Field, I started to take evening college classes, especially Mathematics and English Composition. In my spare time I worked in the base hobby shop, where I built a cabinet for my stereo equipment; I enjoyed this piece of furniture for years after my marriage.

For a hobby, I belonged to the Paine Field search and rescue group. The main focus of the team was to find lost hunters and climbers, which we did on several occasions. There were many climbing outings, including excursions to the summits of Mount Pilchuk, White Horse and Mount Baker in the State of Washington, and to Mount Hood, near Portland, Oregon. I made it only partially up the slopes of Mount Hood, because on this trip I had taken fried chicken that spoiled, and was inflicted by terrible food poisoning. Because I was so sick, I had to stay in the dispensary while the others climbed to the top.

While I was station at Paine Field Air Force Base, my brother Tom, called me from San Francisco, where he was working, wanting some ideas about joining the Air Force. He did end up enlisting, and he spent his tour in Japan.

MY MARRIAGE

Barbara and I met at a party at the NCO club at Paine Field in November 1961. We were married fourteen months later by the military chaplain at the Base Chapel on January 25, 1962. When I married Barbara, I also married her two-year-old son Steve, and from the time I first met Steve, I liked him. I officially adopted him several years later, just before we were to travel to Ecuador. It was important to me that my whole family have the same last name, and for Steve to legally be my son. Tom's wedding present to Barbara and I was a lovely set of bamboo-decorated china dishes from Japan. It was a very good period in my life.

MY MARRIAGE TO BARBARA

On our wedding night and for a few days afterwards, Barbara and I stayed at a motel on Highway 99, north of 112th. For most of 1962, we lived in Apartment C2, 77 Sunset Strip, where Barbara and I managed the apartments in exchange for free rent. I was honorably discharged from the Air Force on June 15, 1962 after 3 years, 10 months and five days employment by Uncle Sam. Our son, Edward, was born on September 1962 at the General Hospital in Everett.

It was a very sad time to be discharged from the services. I would have liked to continue but my job classification as a Machinist was in the surplus category and I was not given a choice in the matter, and Barbara urged me to discharge.

I was able to find work for a short time as a machinist at Triway in Marysville, and at Castle Industries at Paine field. My salary there was $3.25 an hour. Unfortunately, both of these places soon closed and moved their machinery to California. I was lucky, however, and in 1964 I got a job with Western Gear Corporation in Everett where I was employed for almost 20 years.

The site was of a shipyard built during the second war and erected on fill on the waterfront in Everett. I remember during our lunch breaks, we used to fish from the rock bulkhead, and while we ate our lunches we could admire the marine traffic traveling past us in Puget Sound. Because of the shifting ground, however, the machines had to be leveled continuously and, every December, at high tide, water would flood the floors of the shop.

At the best of times, 450 people worked at Western Gear, manufacturing ship deck machinery and cable laying machines. Originally, in Seattle, Western Gear had built gears of all sizes, but later the company purchased a variety of machine shop equipment and diversified. They had heat treatment ovens, welding and assembly shops and a large shop filled with lathes, milling machines, and drilling equipment. They later modernized even more by purchasing numerical controlled tape machines. As for me, I operated a milling machine with a 12' x 40' bed and four milling heads.

At first we lived in a little house on Upper Ridge Road in Everett that belonged to a relative of Barbara's. This is where Paul was conceived.

Here, I remember, we had a cat that ran into the street and got killed by a car. We called Dr. Woods at the Everett Clinic, who was our pediatrician until our kids became adults, and asked for advice as to what to tell them about this tragedy. He advised us just to tell them about it. We did as he suggested, and, after a short period of grieving, everything was OK.

In early 1964, we bought a house at 1715 Goat Trail in Mukilteo. This was the first home both Barbara and I had ever owned. Included with the property was the adjacent lot to the north, and the total purchase price was $12,000, with a $1,000 down payment borrowed from Barbara's Uncle Johnnie and Aunt Isabel, who lived in West Seattle. We paid a mortgage of $80 a month, and $20 a month for the personal loan. Our son Paul was born the first year that we lived in our new home, on November 24, 1964. He is very close in age to his cousin Andrew Beykovský, the son of my brother Tom, who was born in San Francisco on November 12, 1964.

1964

Which one is Paul? The other one is Andrew.

We had another pet tragedy at this house, with a black dachshund named Duchess. The dog went to greet the milkman and unfortunately ran under his truck when he pulled away. Later, we had another dachshund that was run over by the milkman, but luckily this dog survived.

A few weeks after Andrew's birth, Kay and Tom came to live in Mukilteo. Tom got a job with Westin Hotels at the Space Needle in Seattle, and we bought a house on 415 Prospect so that they could live in it. This house cost $14,500, with $800 down, and they paid rent to us to cover the mortgage and expenses.

FAMILY LIFE

Until 1970, Steve and Edward rode the bus to Rosehill elementary school in downtown Mukilteo. I was happy seeing my children attending one school steadily and having friends visiting us in our home, as this was something I never had when I was in school. Jan and Cliff Labaunty and their daughters Lisa and Debbie lived in the house to the north of us. They were lovely neighbors. Lisa and Debbie went to the same school as our children and they spent a lot of time playing together. I was very proud of belonging to my family.

I was also happy digging in dirt in my own backyard, and growing raspberries and dahlias. I had to spend a lot of time controlling the flood in the basement of the house, and renovating in the attic to make extra bedrooms for the kids and us. When I finished the attic, it had one small bedroom to the north and two rooms for the children on the south side. We never painted the outside of the house but needed eventually to install a new roof and a new linoleum floor in the kitchen. My parents helped to pay for that. At that time we had a septic tank, and we had to have it pumped empty continually.

My brother in-law Butch, and his family, also came to visit us a lot. Butch helped me to fix my car and I learned auto repair from him. Many evenings, especially during the holidays, we would play pinochle with Barbara's family. Butch, who had returned from Germany, went to school, thanks to the

GI bill, and eventually became an accountant. For many years he did our income tax and we invited his family to dinner by way of payment for his help.

Barbara's parents Claire and Ora were frequent visitors to our home as well. Claire and Ora lived on Marshall Road in Marysville, in a house with a portable swimming pool. We were very fortunate that they shared the apples, berries and vegetables from their garden with us. They also allowed us to fell some of their trees to use as firewood. From Ora and Barbara, I learned homemaking, and also how to cook and can food. This is where I also learned how to make the best-tossed green salads.

My in-laws were good role models. Several times a year, on holidays, we got together with Barbara's uncles and aunts and their families. I was also fortunate to know Ora's mom and both of Claire's parents. Ora's mom when she was younger, had owned a nursing home, and Claire's mom, Golda, had attended the University of Washington to study mathematics,

Bobbie (Mel's wife) and my mother in law Ora Hathaway   1970

but had to stop when she married Jay, who was at that time employed as a postmaster.

In order to learn about marriage and child rearing, Barbara and I borrowed books from the library, and I watched others to find out about things I hadn't learned when I was a child and teenager. I used Barbara's uncle's families, friends and my cousins in Vancouver as role models.

Mike Hathaway on his 13th birthday. (Barbaras brother)

From Butch and Claire, too, I learned how to fish in the rivers and in Puget Sound. Every year we used to go camping, sometimes to the beach, sometimes to the mountains. We used to pack everything in the pickup, with Steve sitting in the back and the rest of us crammed into the front, and with me as driver. We camped and fished in Newhalem several times, and once in Kamloops, Canada. Another campsite we visited was on the Mountain Loop highway, by the Red Bridge campground.

Another summer, we loaded our Dodge Dart and drove to Canada, where we spent a week in a cabin by a lake and Steve and I fished for trout from a rowboat. There, I remember I got my fishhook caught in Steve's eyebrow. We caught plenty of fish but could not eat it unless it was smoked, as the fish tasted really muddy at that time of the year.

In Washington State, we were lucky to have plenty of natural foods. We dug for clams, which we steamed or cooked as fritters, and we picked wild blackberries, which could be found in the open lots right behind our house, and made them into pies. I also learned to preserve beans, peaches, plums, and to make applesauce. We had a freezer where we could store half a beef (our in-laws purchased the other half), plus other stuff like bread, leftovers, etc.

On several occasions, when Mom came to visit, we made apple strudel together from scratch. First we went to the in-laws and gathered fresh apples; then we peeled and sliced them thin, and kept them in a slightly salted water solution until they were ready to use. The recipe called for egg, lard, flour, salt, lukewarm water, sugar mixed with cinnamon, raisins and coarsely ground walnuts.

The most demanding and fun part about making the apple strudel was the stretching of the dough on a bed sheet on top of our round-oak dining room table. The sheet was sprinkled with flour, and then the dough was put in the middle of the table.

Our hands needed to be constantly dipped into the flour to keep the dough from sticking to them. After lightly rolling the dough to a 1/4" thickness, Mom and I would start to stretch it by getting our hands close to the center of the table and then carefully sliding them out. This way it got paper thin, so thin we could see the creases of our hands through it. Then it was time to put the in the filling. After that Memo would sprinkle melted butter over everything and then we would each raise one end of the sheet and allowed the strudel to roll. This roll was actually long enough to make two strudels, and after carefully transferring them to two cookie sheets, we baked them. Of course it took several hours to make this delicacy -but a much shorter time to eat it! (We had to have tea with it.)

Mukilteo at that time was very small, and Barbara and I liked being part of the 1,000 inhabitants. It was a small town, there was only one gas station, Gene and Bob's store on the comer of Speedway and Casino, and a deli store at the east entrance to the city on Mukilteo

Boulevard. There were wild "cascade" blackberries growing on the hills behind us, and I remember my parents visiting in the summer and as they walked up the hill to our home from the apartment where they stayed in Mukilteo, they gathered the berries for all of us to share them for breakfast.

We enjoyed our summers on the beach and our winters playing in the snow. On rare occasions, because of much snow, Goat Trail Road, which we lived on, and just above our house, was closed to traffic, so the kids could slide down on the icy slope. I did too.

I remember our cars: Barbara drove a Karman Ghia, while I drove a black Ford pickup. I also remember the Taylor Restaurant in the house next to the ferry landing where, in 1961, just after we'd arrived, we had some delicious clam chowder. Mrs. Taylor prepared the food herself and served it at the counter. Later on, "Taylor's landing" was remodeled. Another more expensive restaurant in Mukilteo was the " Seahorse " serving mostly seafood.

In town, we had Larry's Pharmacy, where we opened our first credit account. The Mukilteo Public Library was in a room in a house to the north of Larry's. The librarian lived in the same building in a back apartment, and one year my parents stayed there while Mrs. Fay, the librarian, went on vacation.

When Steve had first started school, Barbara had joined and organized a parents' co-operative. Later on, when all of the boys were in school, she had the opportunity to pursue a part time job. She worked evenings and nights at Madison House, a halfway house for mentally and physically handicapped adults. One weekend, our family and many from Madison House, including two in wheelchairs, went on a picnic to Camano State Park. We dug clams, and cooked and ate them right at the beach. While she worked at this job, Barbara decided to finish her college education, majoring in mental health.

MY PARENTS - BARBARA'S IN-LAWS

The first time my parents came to Mukilteo was before my marriage, while I was still in the service. Later, they came to visit us just about every year. Sometimes they stayed with us in our home, and other times in a motel. They loved to see the children but oddly enough, both refused to learn English so they could talk to them properly.

Of course, it was just as difficult for Barbara to communicate with them, except when I came home from work and did some translating. It was quite a chore for me to both translate and be the middleman between my wife, the kids and my parents. Barbara did her share in going to Everett Community College to learn Spanish, but my parents never made any effort to learn English. I have the sense that my parents knew lots of English, but refused to communicate with others in my family.

My parents usually stayed with us for vacations. Sometimes we'd go camping. When we went, we shared the cost of groceries and gas for the car, because over several weeks, this made it long and they would stay in hotels near our outings. They helped us out by buying because at that time Barbara and I had only enough income to sustain our family and cover our basic expenses. But I also remember bragging and being very proud of having my wife, children, a home, a job, a car and a very good life in the United States, as opposed to the hardships of living in Ecuador.

I know now that Barbara felt totally overwhelmed when my parents came to visit, but my pride did not let me see that. She accused me of taking their side, and I probably did, not knowing any better. Now, in retrospect, I do know better. I should have sided with my partner and wife, Barbara, when there was any conflict or problems.

TWO YEARS IN ECUADOR

I worked at Western Gear, on and off, for a total of more than fifteen years, working as a machinist and as an inspector, including 11 months in 1967 as a first line supervisor. I enjoyed the pay, my co-workers and the management. This was my first steady long-term job after the US Air Force. At Christmas time, we were given a turkey, we enjoyed a yearly employees' picnic, and we had steady jobs without fear of layoff. I traveled twenty minutes from home to and from work and at times worked weekends. For a while I worked the second shift, but neither Barbara nor the kids enjoyed this schedule or the overtime.

Then, in 1970, I was offered an opportunity to work in Ecuador. My brother, Tom, was living there at the time with his family, and he had some friends who worked for Western Geophysical, a company that was involved in oil exploration.

I thought this would be a great opportunity to make an awesome trip and at the same time my parents would get to know Barbara and the kids. Barbara, Edward and I had travelled there for a short visit in 1963, but now it would be an exciting opportunity to take the whole family! I thought that my children and wife would enjoy the stay and be able to visit with the grandparents, aunt and uncle and cousins, so I had no objections to making the trip.

So, we rented out our house in Mukilteo, and since it was for only two short years, I told everyone we would come right back to Mukilteo afterwards. We obtained passports, visas, and vaccinations. With high excitement, I notified Western Gear Corporation of my plans and they told me that my job would stay open for when I decided to return.

Western Geophysical paid the airfare for all five of us, and allowed us an additional cargo of 500 pounds. I went to WGC headquarters in Houston ahead of time to complete the hiring paperwork, and from there I flew to Ecuador. Because I went on ahead, Barbara had the burden of arranging the household for the trip, readying the children and herself, packing, renting the house, and selling my black pick-up and the Dodge Dart we had just purchased.

In retrospect, I never imagined any negative consequences to this journey, or maybe I just ignored the signs that I was beginning to repeat a cycle from my childhood of constantly relocating. As you all know, as a youngster I went many times from home to home, from school to school and from one city to another. I did not realize moving to Ecuador could cause any ill effects on Barbara, the children or myself.

We all had a very nice time in Ecuador. We saw new things that otherwise we would never have had the chance to experience, and my wife and children were able to meet my relatives and to learn Spanish. I was able to show to my family some of the places where I grew up, some of the schools I attended and some of the places I spent in my youth, such as the jungle to the east of the mountains. And of course, they got to see my parents at work in the Pension Pauker and their lifestyle.

But I also realize now that some of the friendships that we had developed here in Mukilteo were interrupted, as well as Barbara's involvement in the community and the pre-school she was participating in. Looking back, if I had to do it again, I would only go to Ecuador for a short vacation with my whole family, rather than making it into a two-year stay.

Once in Ecuador, I stayed at my brother's house until Barbara and the kids could join me. Steve cried with excitement when he arrived in Quito, and I was very happy to see them all. I had already been working in the jungle, and I remember asking the camp doctor to get me some strong medicine for my stomach so that when Barbara and the kids arrived I would be clean and healthy.

The first house we lived in together was near town and around the comer from Hotel Quito, and was protected by iron bars over the windows, doors and outside walls. In this house, we had a maid who'd been recommended by friends. The maid was a black woman, small in stature, very cheery and excellent with our children.

I remember at this time, there was a military coup in Quito, and a curfew was imposed and we had to stay inside. We could see the soldiers in their uniforms walking up and down our street, and later we found out that one of the high ranking military men also lived in our neighborhood. We knew better than to venture out. The next day the maid peeked out and saw there were no more soldiers, it was safe, so we were at last able to go outside and join all the other neighbors.

We next lived in a villa north of Quito on a street called Avenida El Inca. This house was oddly shaped, and the roof, instead of being peaked like a normal roof, was lower in the center. Here is where we were robbed. On our maids day off someone entered the home and stole all the newly purchased gems Barbara had.

Because there was a drought, it was customary for each section of the city to be without water certain days each week. The day before the water was shut off, we would fill up the bathtub and other containers so that we'd have sufficient water for our needs. We had a maid here, too. Barbara taught her to cook, and she looked after the kids when they came home from school, cleaned the house, and washed and ironed the clothes.

At the start of our stay in Ecuador, we didn't do very well financially. The $900 a month salary I was being paid was not enough to cover our expenses. We made a deal with my father to give him $500 dollars, and he would give us local currency in exchange, but I don't remember how many times we actually completed that transaction. He gave us the equivalent in sucres, but we didn't give him our check in dollars. He eventually stopped the one sided exchange, of course.

I had been hired as a mechanic, but I never had to do mechanical work. When I arrived in Ecuador I was told instead to repair engines, but I didn't know anything about engine repair. Very soon, because of my knowledge of Spanish, I ended up doing work as a translator and labor union mediator.

A lot of my work was at the distribution center at the Shell Mera Airport near the entrance to the jungle between Mera and Puyo. The airport was called Shell Mera because early in the 1940's, the Shell Oil Company came to explore for oil, unfortunately they didn't find any. Some of the camps still had the remains of concrete foundations that had been built many years earlier.

Sometimes we flew from Quito to Shell Mera and other times it was a four-hour trip by automobile. It was very exciting to take off from the Quito airport, at 10,000 feet above sea level, over valleys and next to mountains with snowy peaks like Cotopaxi, Tungurahua,

Chimborazo, and Iliniza, and then through a pass to about 1,000 feet above sea level to the airport where we had the distribution center.

At Shell Mera, we had contact by short wave radio to the main office in Quito and also between camps. Trucks brought the cargo in from Quito, and then my job was to oversee the distribution of fuel, food, tools, supplies, explosives and people onto the airplanes and out to the five different camps where the seismic work was being done. The gasoline, which was in 50-gallon drums, and the seismic equipment, which included explosives, were stored away from the airport and were transported and loaded onto the airplanes individually

Salinas, California 1973

Gaby and Victor Beykovsky (our parents) came to visit. At the same time came my brother Tom, his wife Kay and their children Andrew Karen and Jan

for safety. We used a Twin Otter built by the Canadian company De Haviland and an old DC3. The Twin Otter carried up to 4,000 pounds of cargo and DC3 up to 5,000 pounds. We had to be very careful how we loaded everything and we never had an accident or lost any equipment.

During my two years in Ecuador I worked three weeks in the jungle and had one week off in the city with my family. Traveling and crew exchange days were Tuesdays.

I also had a few other jobs in the jungle. I was a substitute for the camp managers when they went to town. I organized the building of two new camps and I directed the dismantling of several camps when the seismic work was finished. None of these places were built as permanent facilities. Built near rivers, the houses were made out of wood milled onsite with a small power saw, the roofs were straw and our water was either pumped from wells or gathered from the rain, and then stored in tanks on towers and heated in steel drums. It was plumbed in for showers, the kitchen and toilets and it all drained into the river.

Men who lived in the jungle, were hired to work on the camps and very few of them spoke Spanish. The crew chiefs that managed and supervised these natives were hired only if they spoke both Spanish and Quechua. The workers were sent to their job sites either by helicopter or, when possible, in canoes made from trees that had been felled and carved out in one piece by the workers themselves. Most of these canoes were about 40 feet long and driven by a powerful outboard motor.

A number of times I worked as a party manager or his assistant. The party manager had a crew on base that included two alternating cooks and four other local employees who cleaned the sleeping quarters and tended to the camp upkeep. There were Australians, British and men from other Latin countries working there, but most of the staff crew, were Americans. Each camp also had an Ecuadorian medical doctor, as well as an accountant, surveyors, a seismic crew and a mechanic.

The work was sporadic and not continuous all day, and the short wave radios were turned off at night, so we had plenty of time to play cards, darts, read, venture into the jungle, fish, hunt and write to our families.

The most difficult time for me was the last week before finishing my three-week term. The long hours waiting for the next load to be shipped from the camp to the distribution center made it very hard to be there. It was even more difficult when I had to stay by myself, with only a couple of the local workers, to close down a camp. I remember I had a Zenith, 11 band, Trans-oceanic to keep me company, and also I always had on hand a short wave radio that belonged to the Western Geophysical, but this was limited to official business only. My fears were probably unfounded, but I had plenty of time to think about possible raids by natives, and snakes or other animals invading my quarters. But these and other fantasies never happened.

During my week off in Quito with Barbara and the kids, we'd have parties at our house, gatherings at other peoples' houses, and we went on trips away from Quito and were visited by my parents who came to see us from Guayaquil.

A couple of times Barbara and I stayed in Puyo while I was doing my job at the distribution center, and we enjoyed short trips into the jungle and along the rivers. Edward also got to join me for a three-week shift in Villano, the nearest camp base to Mera.

We were invited to visit Tom, Kay and their children Andrew, Karen and Ian a few times as well. Tom was by then working as the manager in the Hotel Colon. Interestingly, the owner of this Hotel was the one who had originally hired my parents to manage the restaurant at the Quito Airport in 1950.

In Quito, we met Jim and Becky Sallee. Becky was originally from Stanwood, Washington, and thus began a friendship between our family and hers. The Sallee's had two daughters, Brooke and Storme. The four of us stayed in touch after we all went back to the States.

Later, in California, they lived in Torrance while Jim worked in downtown Los Angeles, and when we were there he showed us his office on one of the top floors of a very tall building. I remember, too, one summer, when the Sallee's came back to visit Becky's parents, we were invited to a salmon picnic at their house in Stanwood. I took my bicycle and Jim and I pedaled to Conway and back. Jim's next assignment, after that, was to some place in Asia, and unfortunately, we lost touch with them.

CALIFORNIA

At the end of my contract with Western Geophysical in Quito, we flew back to Mukilteo and, for a few days, we stayed with Barbara's parents, as our house in Mukilteo had been rented out. I had been promised a seismic crew job with WGC in California, and so we

PAUL AND GABY IN SALINAS

were on the move again, this time to Bakersfield.

We had sold all our furniture at a garage sale before going to Ecuador so we had to buy all new household things in Bakersfield. We bought a stuffed chair, a couch and a dining room table with eight chairs. I started to read seriously while in Salinas, especially interested in John Steinbeck, who wrote a lot about the Salinas Valley, and especially about migrant and farm workers. It was easy to see what he was writing about. The names of the places were still there, such as mountain El Gavilan and Seco River and of-course, Cannery Row.

Then Barbara and I made the decision: we were going back to the Pacific Northwest and our beloved Mukilteo. We saved every penny to pay for our trip home. In early 1974, we rented a U-Haul, packed all our belongings into that and the back of our Chevy pickup, and we headed north. That 1967 Chevy stayed with me until I had an accident in Everett and wrecked it running the red light, driving south on Colby at the intersection with Hewitt.

A SHORT STAY IN MUKILTEO

I was lucky, and, as they had promised, was able to get my old job back at Western Gear in Everett. Nothing had changed, except that I started working as an inspector rather than as a machinist.

We started up our routine at 1715 Goat Trail in Mukilteo again. Paul went to Explorer school, Edward to Olympic junior high and Steve to Mariner high school. Paul and Ed had started competitive swimming in Salinas, but only Paul stayed with it until his senior year at Mariner, to become All America swimmer. Barbara continued to be active with NOW in Everett, and again worked part time in a halfway house for mentally handicapped adults.

MOVING AGAIN, THIS TIME TO EL CENTRO

In mid-1975, I got an offer to work in Mexicali, Mexico, at a Western Gear subsidiary. Maquiladora is a name given to a factory operated in Mexico, usually very near the border, for the convenience of American companies because of the local low wages earned by Mexican natives. These companies are exempt from the labor laws prevalent here in the USA, including health and safety requirements.

We sold both our houses in Mukilteo. Western Gear moved all our furnishings to El Centro, California, where we purchased a house and lived at 1555 Elm Street. I commuted for the duration of the two-year contract, living in El Centro and working in Mexicali.

My job was as general supervisor of a machine shop with three floor supervisors and about 40 shop operators, all of them Mexican nationals. Only management, the electrical department supervisors and I were Americans. I was given a company Oldsmobile with air conditioning, which meant that Barbara got to drive the Chevy pickup.

We had built in our backyard a beautiful swimming pool. We used it many times, even at midnight, because of the hot climate in El Centro. The land in the Imperial Valley, were we lived, was fertile, and produced such vegetables as tomatoes, lettuce, and asparagus, as well as melons and citrus fruits. Alfalfa was harvested six to seven times a year in this valley, as opposed to only twice in the same period of time in Washington State.

In El Centro and neighboring towns we enjoyed the Latin folklore and ate frequently at Mexican and Filipino restaurants. Because both Barbara and I were earning an income, we were able to afford a few more luxuries. On long weekends, we stayed in San Diego and traveled up to the mountains in Mexico and California. Once, we traveled many hours to go skiing on Mammoth Mountain. We also went frequently to Salton Sea, Indio, Palm Springs and Los Angeles. One weekend we ventured south of the border to a resort in San Felipe in Mexico, and another time to Yuma, Arizona.

Barbara learned pottery, organized a NOW chapter and worked for the Imperial Valley Crisis Line. She had a job with the Catholic Community Social Services and, with her friend Barbara Brady, gave presentations about rape awareness in schools and to other local civic organizations.

My job across the border in Mexico had its rewards and its drawbacks. I had a good position as a supervisor, I could practice my Spanish, and I had an opportunity to train many Mexican workers in the American way of doing things. On my daily commute home, I was always able to purchase wonderful, freshly made Mexican corn tortillas. However, one anxiety that plagued me until the day I left was the fear of someone planting marijuana or something similar under my car, so that I would get caught at the border and be falsely accused of smuggling stuff into the US.

El Centro turned out to be a very difficult time for our children. Although Paul learned to play the French horn at his school, and Steve met his first steady girlfriend, Vicky, they had problems in school, and started to smoke. We thought that racism and the social environment was affecting our kids, but in retrospect, I believe moving around as much as we did was the other big factor.

My two-year contract at the Maquiladora was not renewed and so once again, we were on our way back to Mukilteo. At first, the new manager did not want to pay for our move back to Washington, but after a call to the manager who hired me, the new manager changed his mind.

BACK TO MUKILTEO

Our house in El Centro did not sell for a while, which made it difficult to buy another one in Mukilteo. We rented a place on 88th Street and stayed there for three months until, in the end, Western Gear loaned us the down payment to purchase the house at 4803 West Casino, on December 12, 1977, for $48,000.

Our lives were very busy: everyone was attending school, including Barbara and me, on top of our regular jobs. The five of us did manage to spend many of our dinners together as a family. The children learned some basic cooking, and they shared in many of the household chores. For years, we ate pancakes and biscuits that had been made from our own sourdough starter. We canned in jars and made attempts with a food dryer, and rendering lard and we also preserved food in the freezer.

On major holidays, we had picnics together. We also did a lot of traveling: during the summer vacations, we rented cabins by the beach, and pitched tents away from home. I remember we were invited to see the Henrys on Waldron Island, an idyllic place surrounded by soft sand beaches, seashells and driftwood. We went there with the Chamberlins, and spent our time pressing apples to make cider and gathering mushrooms and clams.

In the winter, we rented condos at ski lodges, including at the Mountaineers at Mount Baker and Snoqualmi passes. For many years we went to Mount Pilchuk and other local forests to cut down our Xmas trees. In the fall, we gathered blueberries on the foothills of Mount Baker and Mount Pilchuck.

We got to know other family members better too, visiting the Wilsons, and Barbara's family, and meeting the Kents, who, before moving to Vancouver, live on the Canadian prairies.

I am sure that you, my family, will remember all the other cool things that we did together.

MY TRIPS TO GUATEMALA

In 1976, a year after my father's death, my mother had liquidated the assets of the Pension Pauker and had moved to Guatemala to be with Tom and his family. At first, Gaby stayed in their home, but she was later asked to find her own living quarters. She moved to the Hotel Plaza where she kept an apartment until her death on January 5, 1994. During the last years of her life she had a live-in companion and continued to enjoy the Hotel's garden and its quiet surroundings. Only the sound of the airplanes interrupted this peaceful place, because the Hotel was underneath the landing and take-off flight paths from the airport.

Barbara and I visited Guatemala once together. I made two trips with Helene and several times by myself. My mother also traveled: to Quito to see her friends, to Guayaquil to visit Viktor's grave, to Europe for long holidays with her sister, Dora, and many times she came to visit me and my family here in the US. In the years before her death, I went to see her several times, and in the last period of her life I would phone her on Saturday mornings and chat.

One of the highlights for me on my visits to Guatemala was when I visited Tom and Trudie Hunt. We would usually meet on Tuesdays at the restaurant "La Tertulia" (The Chat) where the Guatemala Friends Service Committee had their weekly luncheon. After retiring several years ago, the Hunts worked at raising money to support and help finance hundreds of Guatemalan native children and young adults who were unable to pay for an education themselves. Originally I met the Hunts while I was looking for Unitarians in Guatemala. Ever since then, I have contributed yearly to their endeavor.

The last time I flew to Guatemala was after my mother's death in 1994. I came back with a few souvenirs, among them a photo album and some knickknacks. Tom had managed Mom's financial affairs after our father's death, and he split the money that was left with me.

END OF MY MARRIAGE

Early 1983, while we were living in the house on Casino Road, the family began to fall apart a bit at the time. The problems we had with our children in El Centro didn't seem to go away. They were bailed out of detention at the police station, and they continued to have bad grades at school. I think, looking back, that the boys probably felt unloved. In spite of this, all three were able to graduate from high school.

Years later, we realized that Steve was mentally ill and we did not know what to do. We tried, but his illness way beyond our understanding. We erroneously blamed his misbehavior on alcohol and drugs; later we realized that drugs and alcohol only aggravated his illness.

By 1980, Steve had moved out of the house and was living at Conquest Center. Paul began working in landscaping, came back home for a short while to live with me, later he rented a house and lived with Debbie, whom he eventually married.

In 1982, Edward married Evelyn, and their wedding was a grand ceremony attended by family members from Guatemala, Canada and many of our local friends. The wedding was at the Mukilteo Light House, with a beautiful view of Puget Sound and the Olympic Mountains in the background.

In the last years as the family still together, all five of us went for counseling at the Presbyterian Counseling Center in Seattle. Unfortunately, I don't remember getting much help at this place. I think the last time I went with Barbara, I was warned by the counselor that a big change was about to occur. Sure enough, the family disintegrated, and I was informed of Barbara's sexual preference for women.

I was now totally out of sync. My family was gone, my household was broken up, my kids were scattered all over Washington

MY FAMILY - 1984

and Oregon, and I did not have the wisdom to seek counsel.

I had several minor accidents driving my pickup, and later a bad one when I ran the red light at the intersection of Colby and Hewitt. Luckily, no one got hurt, but this was when I totaled my pickup. This accident happened when I had Jim Wilbur as a passenger, after we'd spent the evening at a men's rap group in Everett. Of course, my insurance got very high.

My next car was a Toyota. Then I had a green VW, and after that a 1985, 3-door Honda DX which got totaled when someone rear-ended me, and lastly the 1990 Honda DX.

With two student loans, Barbara got her Masters degree in Family Therapy at Antioch College, with an emphasis on Women's Studies. We celebrated her accomplishment.

At the end of our marriage, we each made a list of what we thought belonged to whom and our counselor helped us to split all of our possessions. The Ronda went to Barbara, the pickup to me, and so on, each of us taking a turn until we had divided all we had. Barbara asked me to leave the house the day she came to pick up her things. I went to Guatemala and asked Mom for money to buy Barbara out of her share of the house. Barbara filed for divorce on Whidbey Island, granted there on March 30, 1984.

The year before all of this, Western Gear had closed their doors and moved their machinery to one of their other subsidiaries. I had been earning $15 an hour and I was now unemployed, and by choice for an entire year.

By 1984, though, things were beginning to change for the better. I found work as a supervisor in the numerical-controlled tape lathes and milling machine department at Pacific Car and Foundry in Renton. The salary was good, $3,000 a month. Unfortunately, this shop, too, was going out of business and I was out of work again.

The time, I made myself useful, doing odd jobs for people, and this gave me the flexibility to work my own hours and earn myself a little extra money besides the unemployment check. One job I did was to paint the Wilsons ' house at 550 Eastcot in West Vancouver.

In 1986 I found work as a machinist for Ken Haslin, in La Conner, 35 miles north of Everett. This was a boat and marine machine shop, and I was earning $15 an hour. Unfortunately, Ken went broke. Then, on June 11, 1987, with tens of thousands of other new hires, I started at Boeing Company as an inspector, for $10.48 an hour.

THE FUTURE

Years ago all five of us went to a counsellor in Mukilteo. This was the first time we had attempted to reach out for help. I was told that I did not say things as clearly as they needed to be said. Later, Barbara went to her for information about her affliction with agoraphobia. At that time I had just started to believe that counseling would help. When we lived in El Centro, we had a guest who had a doctor's degree in therapy. I believe he was Barbara's boss or on staff where she worked. Barbara probably told him about my childhood, because he told me that it was a miracle I did not go crazy with all the stuff that had happened to me when I was a child. Anyway, it was a relief to hear that some of those problems were problems that many others had suffered through as well, and that I was one of the lucky ones to have made it to a rational adulthood.

The problem was, when I was a child, I never learned to learn. The way I learn now, as an adult, is by going through the task or the material over and over again. It's the same at work when I'm learning a new process.

My father died on August 17,1975, and Mom on January 5,1994. Mama was very sad that she had failed to bring her mother, Emmy Kende, out of Europe before the war, and she lived and died angry because of it. She was also angry with my father for dying on her. She never forgave the Nazis for killing her mother, and she never forgave my father for dying. She told me that she would never again set foot on German soil because of the Nazi atrocities. Mom was buried in Guatemala City, and Tom was thinking of bringing Dad's ashes from Ecuador to bury him next to Mom and I think that's a nice thought.

In the past years I have cultivated a deep friendship with my Canadian family. Before he died of a heart attack, I met Renate's brother, Uli (Hans) Kent. After his death, Sheila, and her daughters Nona and Stella relocated to Vancouver. Many times, when see the Wilsons, I also visit with Sheila and Stella and Nona and Nona's husband Jim Goddard. Stella currently works for Princess Cruises as a Captain's Secretary; Nona is a published novelist working at UBC; and her husband Jim is a broadcast journalist.

So here we are, Tom and I the oldest, the elders, and the next in line. None of our children are born Jews because, according to Jewish law, the mother has to be a Jew, and because of that, this is where the lineage stops. I think it's an easier way for our children to cope in this racist world. As Mom used to say: "that's destiny".

VISITING THE WILSONS IN VANCOUVER, CANADA

I feel it's important to write a special chapter about my Canadian cousins, the Wilsons. I met the Wilsons for first time in 1959, when I was at Paine Field and they lived on Cypress and the children were small. I was delighted to spend time with them and go with them on outings. I usually arrived on Friday nights and was awakened in the morning by the three kids jumping on the bed, full of excitement. I made the visits continuously, except for a few years when they moved to St. Catherine's in Eastern Canada, and I was working outside Washington State. I missed them very much. But every year I would receive a Christmas card and photograph, sometimes all five of them would be in the picture, sometimes less, depending on who was at home at the time.

The Wilsons became my extended family and an important part of my life. They were role models, which was lacking in my own home when I was growing up. The kids, David, Andrew and Hugh, came into my life just before I started my own family in Mukilteo. It was from them I learned what a family was and how it operated. At mealtime with Jim and Renate, we discussed politics, everyday matters and I learned to do some cooking. For Renate's birthday on May 19, I always brought presents for her from the US, usually a Pyrex bowl or a special dish for the kitchen.

Renate and I went regularly for walks on the trail in the woods near her home in West Vancouver, and we went on many outings in my car to the city, and that's how I learned about the city of Vancouver.

Renate, who never learned to drive a car, was a major influence in my life as a teacher, a mentor and a protector. She constantly informed me about our family matters from all over the world, where she had traveled and visited. She taught me about local and national politics and very thoughtfully protected me from my Mama and Dad's complaints. I am grateful to Renate who changed their opinion about who they thought I was.

Today, Jim and the children and I have a very good rapport and I still visit them frequently. In 1975, when my father died, Renate came down to visit me and assured me that I was going to be OK. She told me not fret too much over the man I called my father and who she called a S.O.B! She requested to my parents personally, while they were all in London, to get off my back and respect me for the good person that I was. When I was down on myself, she would reassure me and remind me what she had told my parents.

I recall humorously that the Wilsons always kept their house fairly cold and, while passing by Jim's study, I would see him all bundled up in blankets while he did his paper work. This is one of my fond memories of my time there.

Renate was a professional writer who published several books: "For The Love of Sports and For The Love of Music"; the biography of a blind family "House Without Windows"; "Inside Outward

Bound", about the famed survival school; and her last, finished posthumously by her family, about Dr. Cass, a physician who spent much of her time in the Northwest Territories, "Thank God & Dr. Cass".

Renate also edited and wrote many articles for local and national magazines. She left many boxes full of her work. She paid for her vacation to Israel with a story she wrote about the kibbutz. Her husband, Jim, worked in city planning, taught at Universities, was a director for BC Hydro and, after retiring, continues to work as consultant. Jim also published a book, "People in the Way", about displaced homeowners who were forced by the government to give way to a dam in Canada.

Their son David, who still has a blanket that I gave him, bought from the surplus store at the Paine Field airbase, and given to him as present, is now a physician; and sons Andrew and Hugh are in business for themselves writing, editing and producing reports, books and other writings. Hugh is married to Nancy and they have a young daughter named Hannah.

My buddy Renate died of cancer on April 14, 1988. Jim is retired, writes and now enjoys lattes down the street from his home in Vancouver.

Visiting Wilsons in Vancouver Canada.

My own sons, Steve, Edward and Paul graduated from Mariner High School, 1978, 1980 and 1982 respectively. Paul was involved in competition swimming in high school and later joined the 'Dolphins' swim team and he was successful in record-breaking speeds in events with his teammates. Paul was honored with the "All America" award in his breaststroke event. We accompanied Paul to many swim meets as far as Oregon, and drove him to practice as far as the Coleman swimming pool, which is an Olympic size containing sea water, in

West Seattle. I would take my bicycle along and while waiting for
Paul to do his practice I rode from the pool to Alki Point and back. I
recall that we were in Anacortes on a swim meet when Mount St.
Helens erupted. We a loud noise from inside the building, and at first
we thought the Anacortes oil refinery had exploded. Both Edward and
Paul took classes in landscaping in high school.

We celebrated with a lovely party for Edward's wedding with
Evelyn Denise White, who was born September 5, 1964. The wedding
guests included many local friends, my brother and his wife from
Guatemala and several Wilson's from Vancouver, Canada. The
ceremony was performed on June 5, 1982, on the front lawn at the
lighthouse in Mukilteo. We had discouraged the wedding because of
the couple's ages, they were under 20, and sadly soon after they
arrived in Oregon they divorced. Evelyn is the daughter of a coast
guard military father.

GEORGE - 1983

I was very active in the pro-choice political arena. I joined the local chapter of NOW. I volunteered at the Women's Feminist Health Center in Everett, on Pacific; I assisted Diane Hale, who was the Director of the clinic, in the lab by cleaning instruments, and for a short time Diane and I dated. This work and the relationship with Diane stopped after the clinic was bombed and burned for a third time, and the insurance and landlord refused to provide further coverage. Fortunately, the arsonist was caught and is now in jail. Other subsidiaries of the organization still exists in Renton, Tacoma and Yakima, and I once assisted, at the Yakima facility.

My involvement with the WFHC was of great benefit to me. I learned about abortion procedures, and heard and understood about the plight of women and their right to choose. I was involved confronting those who opposed abortion and the picketers who disrupted the clinic's operations. I cried with the clinic crew after seeing it burned several times.

Volunteering with the WFHC was the most rewording experience of my whole life. Diane Hale, in matters of feminism, as supervisor and mentor was instrumental in cementing and affirming my beliefs in civil rights.

ALONE AFTER MY FAMILY SCATTERS - 1984

In 1977, shortly after we returned from two years in El Centro, California, we purchased the house at 4803 84th St, SW in Mukilteo, Washington. By 1984, Barbara and I were separated and divorced, shortly before, we asked Steve to move out of the house, as we could not cope with his behavior. Edward married Evelyn and they moved to Oregon. Paul and his friend Debbie moved into a small duplex in the Silver Lake area.

And I was alone. I found a good respite from this loneliness, was and still is, the beach at the Mukilteo State Park. In the past, we had picnics, dug for clams and the kids swam there ever since we lived on Goat Trail. Alone, I would walk from my home down to the beach, taking different routes, to smell the seawater freshness.

On the beach, there's always a light wind and at time a strong wind - excellent for flying kites. Except for weekends, very few people visit this beach. I would sit for hours watching for whales, I saw one, in all those years. I'd watch children play in the sand and gravel and boaters launching in and out of the water. Other times I would walk to the ferry terminal and watch cars and people loading on and off the ferry. For a change, I would ride the ferry back and forth on foot to the town of Clinton and back, and sometimes when I had visitors, they would accompany me. I remember my fishing days and now I'm watching people fishing off the pier. I'm very familiar with Mukilteo and its surroundings, as I have walked the area so many times. I would stop in the Mukilteo cemetery and admire the view from there to the west, across the sound to the Olympic Mountain range. I watched passing dinghies, sail boats, fishing vessels, tag boats and military ships.

I was alone in a house with very few furnishings, and in a way, it was depressing to see the fruits of a marriage fall apart. On the other hand, it was a relief after the years full of discord, as the five of us were confused, angry at each other, and we failed several times in an attempt to get help from professional counselors. I should have never made the move to El Centro, where I got a job with Western Gear Corporation. In retrospect, I believe we should have stayed anchored in the home at 1715 Goat Trail in Mukilteo forever. I see it in my children and grand children, there are benefits of being rooted in one place. It's more convenient and productive for a well-balanced family life and by moving so frequently we weren't able to make those long lasting friendships.

Now in 2004, as I write this, I miss talking about what we liked and what we did not like, when the five of us were together as family. Repeatedly, Steve says he wishes the five of us lived together again.

But as my mother used to say: 'we cannot re-run our past'. When Barbara and I get together, and we do get together frequently, we talk about our shared past life.

I confirmed to myself again in 2005, that we should have remained at our Goat Trail home. I see the benefits for both Paul and his family who live on Camano Island, since Brendan and Nathan were born; and with Edward and his family, who started in Milwaukee and moved only once to where they live now in Gladstone. I see the advantages for those in Gladstone where friends of their children come and go continually, there are church friends, soccer friends and other sports team friends, school and college friends, and Kathy's family who live in the surrounding area. They've created a loving community.

I have come to the conclusion, that in the past when my children were growing up, Barbara and I did the best we could with the parenting skills that we had. Role models where unavailable when I was growing up, as I lived in boarding houses and boarding schools. We lived on farms where schooling was not available, so I was educated away from home. My father told us of a similar life when he was a child. He went to high school in Prague, far away from the farm and his family. He said he disliked it, and, that he would never do the same to his kids, however it happen to him and it happen to me.

In retrospect, as Barbara and I went for counseling both in Mukilteo and Seattle, neither attempt being successful, with the exception of a session where the counselor helped us just before our divorce to divide the household assets between us. We each made a list of items that we thought we had the right to, presented this list at a counseling session and we divided our possessions equitably. I always thought that because Barbara made the arrangements with the counselors I would be at a disadvantage, thus it was difficult to be open to the possibility of a professional helping me.

Looking back, it is difficult to describe the conflict Barbara and I had between us, compounding our ineptitude to deal with our three sons. Moreover, looking back, at that time I did not know how to deal with conflict, and I was not very assertive. We disagreed on most issues related in raising children, thus the conflict. In hindsight, I think we both did the best we could. Barbara completed her Masters degree in Social Work before leaving the family. We were also coping with the difficulty of Barbara's self-diagnosis of 'agoraphobia', the fear of being away from home.

I continued to work at Western Gear, lastly in the quality control department, until it liquidated its business and closed. They sold the property and now in its place a naval base exists. At the time when the community was informed about the development of the naval base, a group of us voiced opposition to build the base.

As the family disruption continued, I did poorly performing my job and I was warned about its consequences. Fortunately, I was one the last ones to be laid off. I was unemployed for a year after leaving Western Gear and earned extra cash by working for friends. I had my toolbox in the back of my car, and did plumbing repairs, minor carpentry and landscaping. I loved this life-style. I loved this life style of being able to choose a time to work and a time to have a good time.

Barbara moved out with her share of furnishing to a home on the south end of Camano Island, and set up an office for her counseling business on the 1200 hundred block of Pacific Avenue in Everett.

I made a trip to Guatemala to ask my mother for $17,000 to pay Barbara for my share of the property we jointly owned. I received the money, paid Barbara, and shortly after, obtained the title to the property. For twenty years, until 1984, Barbara and I jointly owned several homes. Eventually I sold this home in April 1997 for $142,000, originally we purchased the home for $48,000.

It felt very strange the day I received the deed to the property. In a way, I was proud to own a house by myself, but on the other hand, I was lonely in a home that in the past held so much family activity. It looked empty without Barbara and kids and most of the furnishings now gone. Not until months later, did I feel like cleaning and doing house chores, and I was not interested in inviting company over. But in1991, on my 60th birthday I held a party in my house and we celebrated the occasion with Bill Kraemer's retirement, along with many friends from the Everett Unitarian Universalist Fellowship (EUUF).

Soon after everyone left and I was alone, I decided to rent the basement to Dick, I built a bathroom for him and we shared the kitchen, and clothes washer and dryer. His rent was $200 a month and he used my phone until he had enough money to get his own. Dick was recently divorced and sometimes his young son and daughter would come to visit him and at times they stayed over-night. Eventually we became good friends and many times we shared meals upstairs, went to movies, and other events. In the end, he found a women friend and they moved to a townhouse in Lynwood. Before he moved into my home, Dick worked in a bank and eventually got a job in another bank dealing with leased cars. I got my first Honda, a 1990 DX from his leasing company.

Paul came to live with me briefly, and by now he had his own car, a yellow 1951 Ford sedan I called the yellow submarine, and he started working in landscaping, something he learned in high school, and to this day, earns a good living at this profession.

In back of our home was a wooded area where I picked blackberries for many summers to make jam and to eat on top of cereal. Before 1984, I cooked for the children, and baked many goodies for Christmas. I canned vegetables and fruits of the season, made pickles and dried fruit. When my mother came to visit, we made apple strudel. My father who died in 1975, never saw this home.

After being laid off from Western Gear, I was hired by Kenworth Company in Renton for a year, as a supervisor in their machine shop for numerical controlled machines. They manufactured Kenworth trucks. It was the first time I commuted to work and was about an hour each way. After a year on unemployment, I was hired in La Conner, at Beslin's, as a machinist at a boatyard which employed four other people. I discovered it was more fun visiting for lunch and after work in this tourist town.

I was, and I continue to be, a vocal supporter of 'the right to choose' movement. I've had several of my 'letters to the editor' published, and I've participated in marches and rallies. I also was involved in meetings at the Seattle chapter of the Socialist Party, and when they moved to their own location in South Seattle, I volunteered my time to do small repairs and installation tasks on their new building.

For several years, I participated in men's discussion groups which started here in Everett, meeting at the Everett College, later another group at the Edmonds Unitarian Church, and also at the University Unitarian Church. Consequently, this is how I learned about the Unitarian Fellowship on Baker Street, and I have been active ever since in that congregation. I learned much from other men in these groups. I learned how to deal with other men assertively without withdrawing, as I did for years when confronted.

We talked less about sports and work and more about our personal relationships with mates and others. We shared with each other about the difficulties of making friends with other men, and also about the relationships with our fathers; this last issue was always one that took more than one session to discuss. We were profoundly influenced by our relationships with our fathers, even more than relationships with other men or women.

The Everett Unitarian Universalist Fellowship on Baker Street gave me incredible support and friendships. I started going regularly on Sundays, participated as a board member, and learned about sharing and leadership. This is the place where I first discovered and dialogued about my spirituality with others, and cemented some ideas about the religious part of my life. I learned that I don't believe in the after life, and recognize that there is a powerful force in this Universe that keeps us all connected, a connection between things, and all living plants and animals.

For over twenty years while in the Unitarian Fellowship, many things happened in my life such as my divorces, my surgeries, my travels all over the world and especially my personal growth. I called EUUF my home away from home.

When I joined the fellowship, Sunday Services included only 6 to 20 participants, depending on the speaker, it lacked children and children's programs, the building needed upkeep, and it had no functioning board of directors. I stepped up to be president, a job I had for a short period, as I was very incompetent at the time. The few people that attended the fellowship showed interest in rejuvenating the congregation and shortly things got better. We formed an enthusiastic board, made many phone calls, brought in interesting speakers, requested assistance from the UU district office, and we started to expand. I was fortunate to participate in a weeklong workshop, at Fort Warden in Port Townsend, on the Olympic Peninsula, with 20 other Unitarians. The theme was spirituality and leadership. I learned so much about leadership in a church setting, and clarified some of my spiritual and religious beliefs.

Perhaps it was 1986, Paul and I went to the beach in Mukilteo on Father's Day, and I was introduced to Helene Watkins. Helene's son Jim and my son Paul went to high school together, and for a while they continued being friends after graduating. Helene suggested I give her a call to go dancing; I did and we started dating. I lived with Helene until December 1994, when she had movers pack her belongings and moved to her newly purchased home three blocks away. I was shocked about this move because I had no warning of Helene purchasing this property or her intent.

Approximately1986, I traveled to Lenk in Switzerland to visit Mom who was spending the summer visiting with her sister Dora. It was September and the occasion of her birthday. On my arrival to Switzerland, I landed in Geneva and traveled on three different trains to arrive in Lenk, where Dora and Mama were waiting at the station. Dora and her daughter Lore were both still alive and Lore and her husband were also visiting. Mama always talked about her wonderful visits to Lenk and now she was able to introduce me the city. Together we walked the trails, looked for and found mushrooms and wild blueberries, and I even spotted a red fox dashing across an open area in the woods.

The 'Sterne's Chalet', as it was called, was located very high in the mountains, and looked just like Switzerland in the movies. It was about two miles or a half hour walk from the town of Lenk, where many people spoke English. It was a legitimate tourist town. While I was in Switzerland Helene traveled to Australia to visit her cousin.

A YEAR OF MAJOR CHANGES
AND A FRUITFUL START

Thanks to encouragement from Helene, in 1987, I applied for employment and started working at Boeing, only a mile or so from home. I was hired as an inspector and continued in the same job until retirement. I worked mostly inspecting the wings and floors of 747 and 767 airplanes. Almost from the start I was Union Shop Steward and the union representative in my section.

By working at Boeing for almost 10 years, I was able to save enough money, especially because I worked so much overtime, to retire on February 1, 1997. It took an entire year to make the decision to retire, and I because of my nervousness I consulted with a counselor, and also my accountant to ensure I would have enough money. They both concurred with my plan. I also receive a retirement pension from the Union while I worked at Western Gear. The last day of work I had a nice retirement party organized by my co-workers, I was presented with a cake, a leather jacket, a black briefcase, among other presents, and a loving adieu from my co-workers and supervisors.

Helene and I went by car to the San Francisco area and returned driving along the coast back home. Along the way, we stayed, as we had on many other occasions, in youth hostels. On other occasions, Helene and I had stayed at youth hostels in Victoria, Port Townsend, Spokane, Boston, and many others that I can't remember locations or dates. We always reserved ahead for a room and lodged very cheaply while visiting the area.

When I traveled overseas, I also stayed in youth hostels in Jerusalem, Geneva, Vienna, and several in Prague. Accommodations were basic and very economic. Usually there was common bathroom services, clean sheets and blankets with bunk beds in the men's dormitories, and they are usually located near public transportation services. The attendants were mostly local youngsters who were very helpful with directions and other information. It was great to see many so youth traveling all over the world, men and women from different countries, different races, and always willing to talk to me. I was always the grandfather among them.

While in Jerusalem I stayed in the most central youth hostel in town. In the morning we found a huge spread of food such as fruit, breads, lunchmeat and vegetables for breakfast. In the middle of the long table, in several areas they had stacks of paper bags to encourage all to fill them with food for lunch. Many hostels are usually closed from 10 am to 4 pm, and the cost is only $4 dollars a night.

I was also busy learning to fly a Cessna one seater plane, but after fifty hours of solo I became scared and decided it wasn't for me. When landing from the north to Paine Field I flew over our home. For practice, I flew from Paine Field to Renton, Anacortes, and Arlington airports and back.

MY MARRIAGE TO HELENE

There was a conflict almost from the start in my relationship with Helene. In spite of the advice from the counselor to the contrary, I thought a ceremony of commitment would cure all our problems.

On May 25, 1991, at the Evergreen Unitarian Universalist Fellowship (EUUF) in Marysville, Reverend Annie Foerster presided in the union ceremony for Helene and I, which was attended by all our children and grand children. It was a lovely ceremony for which we wrote our own service, and each purchased a ring to celebrate the occasion. For entertainment we had the klezmer band called The Mazletones. Unfortunately, our relationship never improved and in December of 1994 Helene moved out, and in August 1996, my attorney filed a separation agreement.

In spite of it all, Helene and I remained friends and traveled to Spain and Portugal for twenty days. We landed in Madrid and rented a car. We were advised to hire a taxi to guide us out of the city, as the streets were not easy to navigate. I drove, and from Madrid we traveled west to Portugal, south to Lisbon, and to the coast, east to Spain again and north to Madrid. We were enchanted with both Spain and Portugal. We traveled in the daytime, stayed in places a night or

several nights, and used a wonderful guide book written by Rick Steves to plan the details for the journey. We stayed at recommended B&B's, ate where he suggested, and had a successful, happy vacation.

We visited old churches, museums, vineyards, cemeteries, small town day markets, and we had picnics whenever possible. We walked and bathed by the Atlantic seashore, stopped to admire wild fig

Certificate of Holy Union

"What greater thing is there for two human souls
than to feel that they are joined together."

Let it be known by all present that
on the 25th Day of May
in the year 1991
Helene Watkins and George Beykovsky
were joined in Holy Union
at
Marysville, Washington

In witness thereof we set our hands: *George Beykovsky*

Helene Watkins

L. Anne Loretto

Minister, Evergreen Unitarian
Universalist Fellowship
Marysville, Washington

shrubs and cork tree plantations, and paused at religious sites. I was
sad when we had to return. We fortunately did not get robbed, or have
any accidents and we really enjoyed the people in each town and both
countries. I preferred the food and the wines from Portugal over
Spain. Among other sites of world renown, we visited Fatima in
Portugal and the windmills Don Quijote so valiantly fought. For hours
we visited the Madrid Art Museum, and when we needed to rest, we
sat on benches in the town square and talked with the locals.

I was eager to show Helene where I lived while in Ecuador and
we took a trip there. We rented a car with a driver in Quito and
traveled for two weeks. We went from Quito up to Otavalo to a
Saturday market, south to Ambato and Riobamba, back northeast to
Mera, in the jungle, and back to Quito. I was surprised at my own
disappointment as I observed my old home town, with no friends to
see, just memories.

GUATEMALA

Helene and I traveled to Guatemala to visit my Mom and my brother and his family. The last time I saw my mother was when Helene and I went there for her 90th birthday, in September of 1993. We held a birthday party at my brother's house to celebrate. She died the following January. I remember visiting with Kyra and Andrew many times when in Guatemala. Kyra and Andrew are married and now live in Milwaukee with their two children. Andrew finished his training as a PhD in 2005 with a specialty in neurosurgery.

I visited Guatemala many times, also once with Barbara before our divorce, and once with Edward and Helene together. For many years when my mother was still able to walk, she grew and showed orchids. She was recognized for her specially priced species at the annual orchid show in the city.

When visiting my mother, we stayed at the same motel on the upper level where Mom had an apartment for many years. In the last years she had constant assistance from a Guatemalan live-in. At the end of her life, the assistant said that my mother returned from the bathroom, sat on her green chair and passed away very peacefully. My mother and I had talked on the phone every Saturday morning, and several times she mentioned that she was ready to die, that her body was quite worn, and she was not enjoying life any more. She died at 93.

After Gaby died, I received a family album that prompted me to research my family history. My father said nothing about his ancestry and my curiosity led me to research back as far as the seventeen hundreds. I now possess data of nine generations on my my father's side. Now I discovered why my father never talked about his ancestors; Viktor had a rough young life with his dictatorial father and had a falling out with him, and he was a Jew.

Included in the trips to Guatemala was my regular visit with

GABY'S 90TH BIRTHDAY

Trudy and Tom, who were an elderly couple that were dedicated for many years to providing scholarships to Indian children who desired further education. Tom and Trudy were Quakers, and belonged to the Guatemala Friends Service Committee project.

Trudy and Tom had an awesome home in the outskirts of Guatemala City, where I was invited to visit for a vegetarian lunch. We sat on the porch facing a smoking-active volcano, talked and ate vegetarian food. Both were in their eighties and were very well traveled. We discussed their visits and social justice work on the Gaza Strip with the Palestinians in Israel. In Guatemala City, there is a restaurant called La Tertulia, and each Tuesday the 'Friends' held their board meetings and luncheon, and I was happy to be invited to participate. The group held their religious gatherings in Antigua.

Once while visiting Guatemala, we were invited by members of the American consulate to climb an active volcano, with thanks to my brother's connections. Joining us was a Guatemalan armed guard. We were taken in a 'Land-Rover' close to the volcano and climbed on an adjacent twin peak to view the spectacular spewing of lava.

The weather in this semi-tropical climate was always nice and cozy warm, with abundance of fruit such as mangos, oranges, bananas and papayas, just to mention a few, and they were always available and nicely ripe. There was not too much to see except for a neighboring town on Saturday which had the 'market-for-tourists' day. There was also another terrific site at a resort on the shores of a lagoon, and, everywhere there would be flowers blooming continuously all year. The roses were spindly and never went dormant and fuchsias and bougainvillea were always in bloom.

OTHER TRIPS AND VISITS

Helene and I visited with Elsie and Ernest Blaschke in Ontario, and we were fortunate to have Ernest be our guide on a tour to the Canadian side of Niagara Falls. On this trip, we landed in Midway, rented a car, visited with Kyra and Andrew in Milwaukee and drove north into Canada and east to Ontario. We stayed there several days and then returned to Midway airport via Lansing. At that time I learned of Elsie's ill health; she was either in bed or in a wheelchair most of the time.

Several times, with Helene or alone, usually on occasions for someone's birthday, we traveled by car for a day or other times for overnight visits with the Kents in Vancouver, Canada. Together we only visited the Wilsons once, when their son David got married. Andrew and Kyra came to visit and stay with Helene and I, and we took them to La Conner to see the fields of daffodils and the other usual sights nearby. Ben, Debs, Kate and Martin Hofman from London came to visit us and stay at my house. They saw some Northwest sights, and we went for an outing at Camano State Park with my son Paul and his family. From Scotland, Sue Bell, a cousin on mother's side, came to visit, and we had a picnic on Camano Island with Paul's family.

Paul and Debbie were married in a lovely ceremony at Forest Park in Everett on September 30, 1990.

ODDS AND ENDS

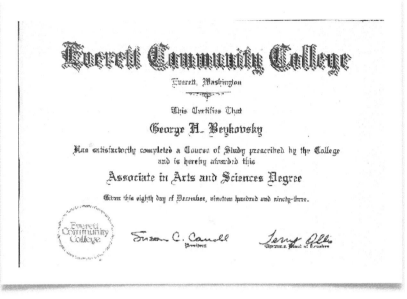

GEORGE'S COLLEGE DEGREE

I worked very hard to earn an Associate Degree in Liberal Science at Everett Community College. I graduated in June 1994, with a 3.1 GPA, after spending over 20 years of accumulating credits from classes that I took mostly in the evenings. I enjoyed both math and drawing classes and I had difficulty with English and History.

At the Everett Community College, I volunteered at the Refugee Forum interpreting English/Spanish at several elementary school parent-teacher conferences. I met

Elodia and Nellie who also interpreted Spanish there. I continue my friendship with Elodia to this day, and we get together periodically, especially on a school break, as she attends the University of Washington to study for her Masters in Social Work.

In 1996, together with my sons Edward and his wife Kathy and Paul his wife Debbie, I attended a Frohlich family reunion, on my mother's side, in the Czech Republic. Fifty-one members of the family attended this important event. We visited the Terezin distribution camp, and among approximately 80,000 names we read the names of a couple dozen family members on my mother's side that were murdered in the Holocaust.

We also visited Zabreh (Hohenstadt) where in 1725 our ancestors lived and owned an alcohol distillery. Participants at the reunion came from Australia, Austria, Canada, France, Ireland, Italy, Scotland, UK, US and Switzerland. There was not one participating family member that at the time lived in Czech Republic. Several members of the family visited their own homes or farms where they, their parents, or relatives had lived before the War. We met many of our family members for the first time. Some of us never knew of others, and I finally had the chance to build a reliable family tree.

We had a family member who found this opportunity to explain the family's tragedy in the Holocaust. One member of the family interviews the head of each household and records their stories. This was an intense ten-day journey full of tears and laughter and I still keep in touch with all participants and periodically re-read their stories. I have since visited the relatives I met in Prague in their own countries after this family reunion, and I finally feel like I belong.

Most importantly, we were horrified to learn of the final days of my grandmother Emmy Kende. Of all those from my family who perished in the Holocaust, Emmy is the only one I knew personally. In 1939, before we left for Ecuador my mother begged her to come with us to Ecuador. My mother's three sisters also begged her to leave Olomouc in Moravia, where she lived with her sister. Emmy said, "Why would I leave when I never meddled in politics and why would the Nazis bother with a 75 year old innocuous person? And besides that, I would be a burden to you all. I'll just stay."

We verified that Emmy Kende from Olomouc was deported October 15, 1942, to Terezin and consequently to Treblinka extermination camp. After the family reunion my son Edward returned to his home in Gladstone, Oregon and told Emmys story to his children. His fifteen-year-old son Adam was so moved by the story that in 1997 wrote the poem below.

ADAM BEYKOVSKY

MY GRANDSON ADAM TALKS ABOUT MY GRANDMOTHER EMMA KENDE

A TRUE STORY

My family has been through the Holocaust,
Some have lived and others lost.
My grandpa was the lucky one,
For he went on to have three sons.
He left at age eight
Never to see his grandma again.
You see she thought she'd be OK,
So she stayed behind to live her way.
A patch of yellow on her arm,
They took away her house and farm.
They send her to the Terezin,

182

This is where her life ends.
Thousands lost their lives that way,
And others lived another day.
My dad and mom went back to see,
What was left of family.
They've all moved on,
All those who lived.
But came back to the family reunion.
There was lots of tears and joy that week,
All friends they made
They know they'll keep.

By Adam Beykovský

1994 TO THE PRESENT

1994 was a year of many changes in my life. My mother died early that year, my cancerous prostrate was removed in June, I earned my Associate in Liberal Arts Degree from Everett Community College, Helen and I traveled to Europe, and in December 1994, Helene suddenly moved out to her newly purchased home, a couple blocks away. Then I shaved my beard for Christmas!

I lived in Mukilteo until August 26,1999, which is the day I moved to Everett ,Washington. I purchased my condominium for $218,000. It was a big change from caring for the garden, lawn, maintenance and repairs of a house, to only caring for the inside of my new home. The condo owners all share the outside maintenance by paying monthly dues. After the inspection, it took very little to

GEORGE AND ADDIE MINNICH

persuade me to buy it and since I purchased it directly from the owner, I saved ten per cent of closing costs.

My lifestyle changed drastically after moving to a condo, now that I was living in Everett, I was close to my bank, favorite restaurants, and the post office. I was in close proximity to the buses to and from Seattle, my favorite city, and to the train station to Vancouver, Canada.

I repainted my apartment and refinished all the woodwork. Shortly after I moved in, I purchase a new hot water heater, dishwasher, clothes washer, and refrigerator. I'm thankful to Addie Minnich for informing me of the availability of Unit 204. We attend the same church in Marysville, and one Sunday she mentioned that a unit was available for purchase. Sadly, Addie died July 2, 2002, of heart failure.

On two different occasions, at the Unitarian Fellowship, I was a part of a committee to search for new Minister and we selected Amanda Aikman (1996) and Alicia Grace (2001).

An important experience that serves me well is my volunteer hours on the telephone at the 'crisis line' here in Everett. I was very well trained by my supervisor Judy to go on line, and I worked there from Fall 1996 to mid 2000. I usually worked four hours shifts once or twice a week and was trained by excellent social workers.I made several friendships that lasted while I worked there and a few friendships that I continue until today. While I visited Prague, Judy joined me for one week. She was one of my trainers and supervisors at the crisis line. Judy worked for three years in Ukraine on contract with the Peace Corps teaching English there. Another supervisor and trainer at the crisis line was Kate. Kate's daughter Jessica lived and studied in Ecuador, and Kate invited me to go along to visit with her. This was my first visit to Cuenca, an old town in the south of Ecuador. We walked a lot, visited old churches, the open-air markets, old Inca ruins, and ate their grand food.

I met Ted while volunteering at the Crisis Line, with whom I have stayed friends with until today. He teaches computer science at the Edmonds Community College and I visit with him there, almost regularly, for lunch on Thursdays. He lives with wife on Whidbey Island, in a lovely home on a 40-acre parcel, where I am invited for lunch occasionally when he is not teaching. I also get the benefits from his vegetable and flowers garden. In 2005, Ted retired from teaching and now, as hobby, besides tending to his property, he sings in a maritime choir on Whidbey Island. He has traveled to several countries in Europe with the group to perform.

POSTSCRIPT

I have succeeded in making a good life for myself and I am fortunate to have my family Barbara, Steve, Edward and Paul live close by. I live in Everett, Washington and my favorite friends also live close. I visit with Barbara, my children and grandchildren often and I like to baby-sit my grandchildren.

BARBARA is a successful Family Therapist and lives by the beach, she has a garden and pets on Camano Island, and, with whom I continue to have a very important friendship and I respect. We see each other many times a year and we talk about our children's matters. I really believe, with all my heart, that while we were together, each of us did the best we could with the information we had learned from the past.

STEVE lives independently in Everett and is successfully learning to manage the ups and downs of a very difficult mental illness. Schizophrenia.

EDWARD, and his wife Kathy and their five kids live in Gladstone, Oregon. He has a sales position at his job, and an extensive involvement in sports with his children Amy, April, Adam, Alyssa and Ashley. Kathy is an insurance agent.

PAUL, his wife Debbie and their two kids live on Camano Island. Paul is also successful, working as an independent landscape contractor. Debbie works raising their children Brendan and Nathan, and she is an artist that draws at home and is also a wonderful photographer.

I love and I am very proud of Barbara, Steve, Edward and Paul and their families.

MAY ECUADOR REST IN PEACE AND I GO ON

I wrote this biography so you, my children and grandchildren, might understand better about who I am. I am an accumulation of living 8 years in Czechoslovakia, 18 years in Ecuador, and more than 61 years living in the United States from 1957. Most importantly since 1962, with you who became my dear family.

With deep love and never a regret. George.

CHAPTER 4

My Ancestors

SAMUEL BEYKOVSKÝ OF SCHWENDA/SVETLA

Born about 1719, and died at age 90. He married Katharina Polacek. I rather think the mother of the children was Anna who was described as Samuel's wife in 1793. The information we were given, which has not been validated is that Samuel married Katharina Polacek on June 16, 1794, if so that would be his second marriage, and they had five children: Herman, Anna, Magdalena, Bernard and Lazar.

BERNARD BEYKOVSKÝ 1763-1830

Bernard Beykovský was born about 1763, he died August 18, 1830, in Strechov at age 67. He was a tradesman and butcher. He married Sara, the daughter of Samuel Pozer and the wife was Lidmila from Cabelic.

Records show they had ten children:

Lidmila born on March 15, 1801;
Abraham died as one year old child December 14, 1802;
My ancestor **Jacub born June 3, 1804,**
Rosarie born January 2, 1807;
no- name child still born March 15, 1808;
Josef born July 26, 1809;
Salamon born August, 24, 1811;
Mojzis born August 20, 1813;
Anna born July 3, 1814; and
Marie born August 10, 1816

JACUB BEYKOVSKÝ 1804-1881

Born June 3, 1804, in Lhota in the Jewish Community of Kacov and died August 27, 1881. I know very little about Jacub Beykovský and wife Anna Baumann except that on the birth certificate of their son Josef Beykovský it shows where it identifies his parents, and also I found a reference to Jacub as he purchased the seats in the synagogue in Pitcovitz. (As per Hugo Gold, 1934)

On April 2005, I received from the office of Czech archives the confirmation that Jacub and Anna had four children: Rosalie born 1832, Adolf born 1833, Josef born 1834 and Nathan born and died 1842.

ANNA BAUMANN 1808-1884

Anna was born in Weldruby in 1808 and she married Jacub Beykovský in 1829 in Cestin,. She died on March 29, 1884.

M. BAUMANN DIED 1869

Photo provided by Eva Lisková: Anna in 1863

ROSALIE (NEE BEYKOVSKÝ) POLLAK, 1831-1891

Rosalie Beykovský was born 16 August 1831 and on October 2, 1853 married Jacob Löbl Pollak from Bistriz, Bohemia. Jacob was the son of Löbl Pollak, a 'spirit maker'. Rosalie died September 12, 1891.

Photo provided by Eva Lisková.

(Rosa) and Jacob had nine children: <u>Aloisa</u> married William Kreitner and she died in 1912; had no children. <u>Klara</u> married Adalbert Oplatek and she died in 1916 had no children. <u>Berta</u> married Alfred Gärtner and had eight children; both died in the concentration

194

camp. <u>Gottlieb</u> died at 21 years of age. <u>Leopold</u> (Poldi) 1861-1911 married Camilla Kohn 1870-1939; had five children. <u>Emil</u> b.1863 married Karoline Fuchs 1874-1936, had no children, <u>Heinrich</u>, <u>Hugo,</u> and Rosalie's twelfth child Ottokar, was born 1870; she was 38 years of age when the last child was born.

I have to thank profusely Pat and Roy Trumbull for connecting me to the Pollak family, particularly with Gracie Polk. By the way, Pollak (Gracie's ancestors) changed their name to Polk in 1938. I visited Gracie in New York   ce provided me a copy of the letter from her father Harry describing details about their family ancestry, also I have a copy of the cookbook written by Rosa Pollak, some valuable photographs and connections to other members of the family in the Pollak branch.

The typewritten letter dated October 8, 1971, by Harry Polk (Hans Gunther Pollak) is addressed to Gracie. Both in the letter to Gracie and the cookbook identify us as originated from same ancestors. In the letter Harry describes all the members of the family from Rosalie Beykovský down to when he finished the letter in 1971. Harry died in 1983 in Vienna, Austria.

See the Letter to Gracie and the photograph of Gracie in New York.

ADOLF BEYKOVSKÝ, 1833-1871

Adolf Beykovský, born about 1833 married Rosalie Fischl from Kuri and he died about 1871. For years both Peter Lowe and I were skeptical about Adolf actually being a son of our common ancestor Jacub Beykovský, however Peter was always more of an optimist. In 2005 we received confirmation from Czech archives that Adolf was in

Pitkovice farm house being built near Uhrineves. Farm land was leased originally by Josef Beykovsky and managed by son Vilem, in the production of grains and fine horses. Siblings Anna, Gustav, Otto and Vilem were born here. Eventually September 1942, Vilem and family were ordered to appear for deportation, Vilem was found dead of self-poisoning, that morning.

Vilém Beykovský
(Pitkovice)

Josef Beykovský

Photos before 1934.

196

fact the son of Jacub, thus my kinship to Peter Lowe.

JOSEF BEYKOVSKÝ 1834-1921

This is where it all started in 1994, after my mother died.
Below is one of the photographs that was included in the album she so

ČESKÁ REPUBLIKA

Č. j. 1/95

RODNÝ LIST

V knize narození (rodné matrice) matričního obvodu
Suchdol, okres Kutná Hora

svazek......**F**......., ročník...**1834**......, strana......**79**......, poř. č. .....**6**...... jest zapsáno

Den, měsíc a rok narození		22.12.1834 – dvacátý druhý prosinec jeden tisíc osm set třicet čtyři
Místo narození		Bečváry, část Červený Hrádek
Jméno a příjmení dítěte		Josef Beykovský
Pohlaví		mužské
Otec	Jméno a příjmení	Jakub Beykovský
	den, měsíc, rok a místo narození	neuvedeno
Matka	Jméno a příjmení	Anna roz. Moisesová
	den, měsíc, rok a místo narození	neuvedeno
Poznámky		-----

V Suchdole

Dne 22. prosince 1995

matrikářka

EVT - 03 002 0 - Rodný list pro cizinu   II/95   Tiskárna KOČKA 2409/9?

JOSEF'S BIRTH CERTIFICATE

carefully and lovingly put together, written in 1915 by my father addressed to his grand father Josef Beykovský. The post card shown below originated in Pitcovitz. This is the first time I heard about the name Josef Beykovský and the name of the town. As I was told very little about my paternal ancestry I decided to search my ancestors and the results of over ten years of search are contained here.

My great grand father Josef Beykovský was born 12 December 1834, in Becvary, Bohemia and he died of old age in the Prague sanatorium September 25, 1921. He married Louise Dubsky November 11, 1863. She was born in Luonovice, Bohemia 12 September 1843, oldest of 12 siblings and died at 6 AM May 9, 1909 in Prague.

They lived in a suburb of Prague named Kral Vinohrady, Karlova St #20. Her death certificate has the address in Czech. The address on my father's postcard to Josef is addressed in German. Still to today, many names of places on maps are written both in Czech and German.

NATHAN BEYKOVSKÝ, 1842-1842

This information implies as still born or died within the first year of his life.

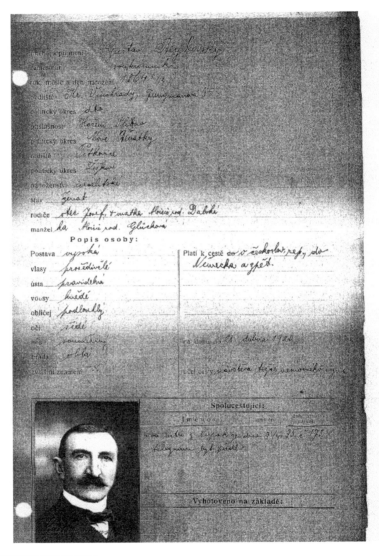

GUSTAV'S REGISTRATION

GUSTAV BEYKOVSKÝ 1864-1929

Gustav, my grandfather, was born December 06, 1864, in Pitcovitz and died November 14, 1929, in Prague. Gustav's death date is contained in a court deposition where my father Viktor claims his inheritance of 1.185.00 Kc - which he never received as the monies were embezzled by cousin and lawyer Siegfried Vitezslav Kersch.

My brother Tom and I made our first pilgrimage together to the

My grandfather Gustav Beykovský's Family census

Czech Republic and the most exciting part of the journey was to visit the archives in Mlada Boleslav, near Horny Slyvno, the center depository of old documents. Here we obtained a copy of a 1900 census page #38 about the Beykovský family; in it includes Gustav, Louise, Otto and Karel.

The entry for Gustav includes his birth as December 6,1864, in Pitcovitz, and that on May 1, 1891, he leases a farm from Count Kolovrat in Horny Slyvno, District Mlada Boleslav, which includes 134 bovine and 4 horses. Gustav is barely 27 years of age when he leased the farm. This is the extent of my knowledge about my grandfather, except references that my mother made in her biography located within this book, in the section titled, From Innsbruck to Ecuador-Memoirs of Gabriele Beykovský.

My grandparents, Gustav and Louise married in Franzensbad, Bohemia on June 4, 1895. Louise's parents are Markus Glück and Nelli (Jetti) Stein.

My mother told me many times that her in-laws, the Beykovský, were dictatorial, stern and although not religious, were set in their Jewish traditions. My father had nothing to say about his father, except that he regretted being sent away from home at age 10 to study in Prague. He wished otherwise for himself and later for his own children, but that wish was not to be.

Accompanied by his mother, my father Viktor and his two brothers were sent away from their home to attend school. I deduce that Gustav stayed alone in Horny Slivno caring for the farm. Before he died he entrusted his money to Vitezslav Kersch who embezzled (1.185.000 Kc) my father's inheritance.

LOUISE GLÜCK 1867-1929

Louise, my paternal grandmother, was born December 28,

Louise's train pass in 1913

1867, in Lundenburg (Breclav), Moravia, and according to the same 1900 census she arrived at the farm in Horny Slyvno, about 50 kilometers north of Prague, on June 1, 1895. She married Gustav. My father Viktor mentioned, with shine in his eyes, that he learned the piano by sitting at the piano bench with her, watching her play continually, especially Czech national folk songs. My father never learned to read music.

LOUISE AND VIKTOR IN PITCOVITZ - VIKTOR WRITES TO HIS GRANDFATHER JOSEF.

Viktor shared, with his future mother-in-law Emma Kende, that his mother Louise had died about the same time he had met Gaby in 1929. The earliest photograph I have of Louise, is her issued train pass from 1913, (see below) with her photo on one side. I assume that both Viktor and his mother Louise moved from Horny Slyvno to Prague in 1913 to pursue his high school studies.

OTTO, KARL, VIKTOR AND LOUISE 1911

Gustav and Louise had three sons: Otto, Karl and Viktor and they were all born on the farm in Horny Slyvno. Otto, the oldest sitting on the chair, Karl standing, and Viktor next to their mother.

OTTO BEYKOVSKÝ 1896-1916

Otto, the eldest of three sons, was born April 16, 1896, in Horny Slivno District Mlada Boleslav in Bohemia. He was in the army as second lieutenant in reserve and died as a soldier, barely over twenty years of age, in WWI on October 3, 1916. He is buried in the cemetery of Pomorzay District Zbarow in Galizien-now Ukraine. Census shows Otto as a student in Prague at age 10. Otto died in 1916 fighting for his country as a soldier.

My mother tells a story told by my father about Otto returning

OTTO'S BIRTH CERTIFICATE

home in an elegant and new military uniform he was given after finishing his basic training as a military soldier. They were at the dinner table, and Otto was sitting at his father's right side, and as he was talking to his father he leaned his elbow on the table. The father was so outraged, that he grabbed his son's arm, and smacked it hard on the table, as he said in a loud voice, 'Even you as a military officer will not disrespect me in my house by putting your elbow on my table'.

Below is a memorial plaque displayed in the hallway in Horny Slivno elementary school.

The inscription reads:

FALLEN SOLDIERS
-Thirteen names follow-
GAVE LIFE FOR OUR FREEDOM

Jméno a příjmení:

Podpor.

Otto

Bezkovský

Narozen

Příslušnost   země

                                    země

Umrtí

Země

Pohřben

Místo   hřb.   řada
                                   odd.   čís. hr.

Založeno   země

          svazek   čís. poř. hřb.

4/76   čís. poř. dokl.

Opsáno na podkladě

Adresa pozůstalých

KARL BEYKOVSKÝ 1897-1929

Karl, the second eldest son, was born April 23, 1897. He joined the army February 1, 1917. According to a letter from Martin Luther University Halle-Wittenberg in Germany, Karl attended college from October 6, 1919 to February 5, 1924, where he studied farming. I

KARL'S BIRTH CERTIFICATE

assume that Karl died before the year his father died, in 1929. I have not located his death/burial date or burial site to confirm this.

Mentioned in the Vienna census dated March 20, 1922, District 16, 6 Herhardt St, lists Karl as a College Student.

VIKTOR JOSEF BEYKOVSKÝ 1902-1975

1908   1908   1917

My father Viktor was born March 21, 1902, in Horní Slivno, northwest of Prague, then the Habsburg Empire. School records from Dolni Slivno reflects his grades as an average student and a Jew. He was 53 half days absent in his first year of school and 28 absent days the second year.

On a train from Prague, I arrived at Slivno whistle-stop train terminal and walked about half an hour up the hill to their family farm. I visited the location of the farmhouse and noticed many lilac bushes in the front yard surrounding a pond. I asked several people about our surname Beykovský, and was told that many people worked for the "Jew" but they did not recognize the name; however they mentioned that one of the sons was killed in WWI. Otto was killed in that war and I assumed they were referring to Otto.

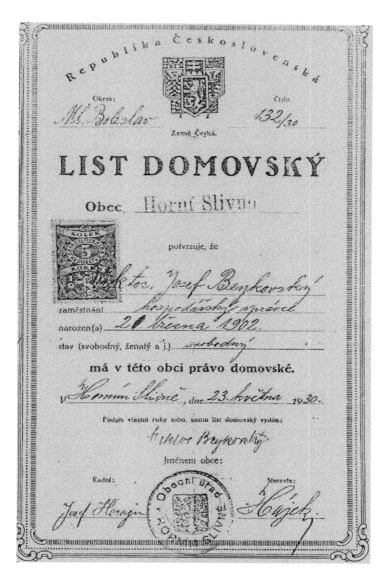

VIKTOR'S BIRTH CERTIFICATE

Viktor Josef Beykovský married Gabriele Kende on June 24, 1930. Witnesses to the occasion were his uncle Vilem Beykovský and Marie Mändl, the wife of the farm owner. Marie, by the way, is Gabriele's aunt. The newly married couple went on their honeymoon

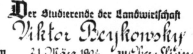

Der Studierende der Landwirtschaft

Viktor Berykowsky

boren am   21.März 1902   zu Ober-Slivno

t am   25. Juli   1925 die Diplomprüfung gemäß der

:üfungsordnung vom 24. Juli 1922 mit dem Gesamturteil

„gut"

bestanden.

Auf Grund dieser Prüfung wird ihm hiermit der Grad _____

Diplomlandwirt

verliehen.

le a.d.S., den 4. August 1925.   Der Dekan

VIKTOR'S DIPLOMA

to Dubrovnik on the Adriatic Sea in Yugoslavia. Afterwards, Gabriele and Viktor had a small apartment in the estate house, but Viktor was anxious to be independent and on his own.

By now Viktor realized that his inheritance was decimated by the lawyer's habit of gambling on horses. With the little money he had left and moral support from his uncle Vilem, Viktor and Vilem traveled to Slovakia, where renting a farm was cheaper and found and leased the farm Sabatka Pusta. It was here since 1931 that Viktor and Gaby farmed, had two children and lived until their departure to Ecuador in 1939.

On the farm Viktor grew beets for the production of sugar, and fodder for his farm animals and for the military cavalry garrison next door. He raised horses, pigs, goats and chicken and my mother grew vegetables for home consumption. The farm was located in an area with four yearly seasons, they grew everything including grapes, apples and pears. On every occasion possible, my father went to Rimavska Sobota, a town about three Kilometers from the farm to enjoy his favorite pass time, playing cards. He mentioned to me that he learned to smoke in Kocvar to combat the strong smell of horses and pigs.

Viktor was very happy with a steady job, a new family and plenty of relatives that came to visit during harvest time. My mother mentioned her utter happiness at the farm, and the visits from her mother Ema and many cousins.

My father never had company visit from his family. At harvest time, besides the joy of visits from my mother's family, my father engaged many Hungarian laborers to work at the farm. The farm was a few kilometers from the Hungarian border and Viktor regretted the visits from the gypsies during the harvest, because they came more for handouts and stealing, rather than for employment to earn their keep.

The last opportunity to visit with my father in Ecuador was March 1975, and after a battle with cancer, he died on August 17, 1975. Viktor's tombstone reads in Czech: ZDE ODPOCIVA VZACNY CLOVEK (HERE RESTS A RARE HUMAN BEING) 21-III-1902 17-VIII-1975

El hogar Beykovsky Kende está de luto

La muerte de un ser querido, más que de él es nuestra, puesto que nosotros la vivimos.

P. B. M.

El día 17 de Agosto, el Hogar Beykovsky fue visitado por el Angel de la paz, con la separación del apreciado señor VICTOR BEYKOVSKY GLUCK.

José Beykovsky nació en Horny Slivno república de Checoslovaquia el día 21 de Marzo de 1902. Realizó sus estudios primarios, secundarios y superiores en la misma ciudad, habiéndose incorporado de Ingeniero Agrónomo. Luego contrajo matrimonio con la gentil dama GA-

BRIELA KENDE, también checoeslovaca.

Formaron un hogar saturado de amor, paz y buenas costumbres, recibiendo de Dios, como recompensa de esa generosa fusión de almas, dos hermosos hijos: Jorge y Tomy, que han colmado de gloria y honor a sus padres.

En Julio de 1939, el señor Beykovsky, en calidad de Ingeniero Agrónomo, emigró al Ecuador. Se estableció en Ambato, administrando varias haciendas en Ambato y Cayambe durante doce años. Su tónica característica en esta administración fueron su honradez y dedicación al trabajo.

En 1951 se trasladó a Guayaquil para trabajar con Panagra, luego se independizó para trabajar por su propia cuenta en la Pensión Pauker hasta cuando le llegó su último día.

La muerte no le tomó de sorpresa. El pudo realizar la cercanía del momento supremo. Tampoco le tomó miedo, pues su vida fue de un hombre honesto, trabajador infatigable y

fiel a sus principios religiosos. Sus manos estuvieron siempre abiertas al necesitado, el dinero no fue un patrimonio egoístico para El, ya que supo siempre compartir con sus semejantes, el alcance de sus posibilidades.

Su muerte serena fue un reflejo de lo que fue su vida.

Su sencillez quiso llevarla hasta la tumba. Dispuso se lo enterrara en cuatro tablitas a lo natural y en tierra. Su Señora cumplió su mandato de la máxima austeridad y sencillez, rodeado de los amigos más íntimos, recibió su último ADIOS traducido en la plegaria de sus familiares y amigos.

Víctor José ya habrá recibido la recompensa prometida a aquellos que dieron pan a los necesitados, vestido a los desnudos y amor a los que carecían de él.

Paz en tu tumba, querido Hermano Víctor y consuelo y resignación para los tuyos.

LEVANTATE — 17

VIKTOR

216

GABRIELE KENDE 1901-1994

My mother Gaby, as she was called by my father Viktor and her family, was born on September 12, 1901, in Innsbruck, Tyrol, Austria. She's the daughter of Emma Fröhlich from Hohenstadt, Moravia, and Ignaz Kende from Nagykanizsa, Hungary.

Gaby wrote her own biography including up to the time Viktor died. I asked her many times to complete her biography, but refused

GABY AS A BABY AND A TEENAGER

to do so, saying that she did not wanted to recollect the times after she became a widow.

Gaby always reflected sadness and anger over what she called 'what life dished out to her'. Many things in her life were disappointing for her. She was the youngest of four sisters. Her three sisters were allowed to attend prep school, but when the time came for her to go, her mother was practically broke. So Gaby had to go to Germany and work as a nanny, rather than attend a prep school.

Then in 1939, the Holocaust forced her to leave the comforts and security of a home and her extended family living nearby. She painfully lost her mother Emma to the gas chambers, and she had to travel to an unknown country in remote, primitive South America. Gaby and her family were very poor for the first ten years living in Ecuador, since immigrants were only allowed to be employed on farms. She lived and worked in homes without hot water, indoor plumbing and poor lighting. Butter and other essentials for cooking were non-existent, and for the first time in her life, she had to scrub her

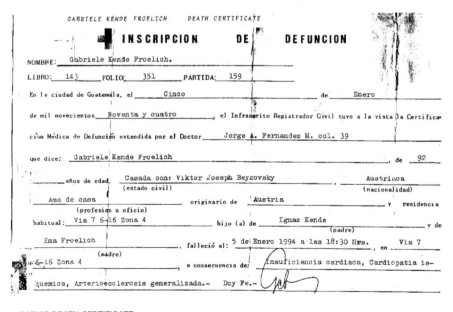

GABY'S DEATH CERTIFICATE

own floors, cook her own meals, wash her own clothes and find a part time job to earn some money.

Gaby always remembered the years on the farm in Slovakia as the happiest of her life especially after her first son Jirko Harry was born August 22, 1931. On the farm, the delivery was assisted by a midwife and grandmother Emma was also present. Although she lost a succeeding pregnancy while riding in an auto, she later bore her second son Tomas Jan on February 19, 1936.

While her children were growing up, my mother had the loving help of the farmhands, the cooks, and especially of Gazda, the farm foreman, who took it upon himself to care for young Jirko. He took the child along on his farm duties and errands.

Gaby died of old age on January 5, 1993, in Guatemala City, Guatemala.

JIRKO HARRY BEYKOVSKÝ 1931-

I was born August 22, 1931, at 10:30 AM, on Sabatka Pusta farm, Slovakia near Rimavska Sobota. I have no memories of my life on the farm except for anecdotes I was told by my parents, as an adult.

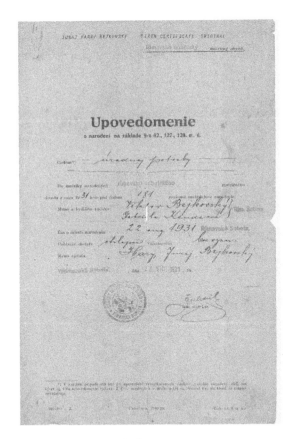

JIRKO'S BIRTH CERTIFICATE

TOMY AND JIRKO 1936

My mother explained to me about the farm, as we were looking at the photographs, and this is the extent of my knowledge about my childhood. I believe the reason for my lack of memory is a result of the drastic change of moving from Europe to South America. My first real memories I can recollect are written in my chapter about Ecuador, soon after I started third or fourth grade in school in Quito, Ecuador.

TOMAS JAN BEYKOVSKÝ 1936-

Tomas was born February 19, 1936, on Sabatka Pusta farm in Slovakia. He was not even four years old when our family was forced to depart Slovakia in 1939, because of Hitler's racism and the

TOMAS IN 1937

holocaust.

č. 673/1996

RODNÝ LIST
V knihe narodení matričného obvodu
Rimavská Sobota

zväzok 8   ročník 1936 strana 216   por. č. 36   je zapísané.

Deň, mesiac, rok narodenia a rodné číslo	19.2.1936-devätnásty február jeden-tisíc deväťsto tridsaťšesť neuvedené
Miesto narodenia	Rimavská Sobota
Meno a priezvisko dieťaťa	Tomáš Bejkovský
Pohlavie	mužské
Otec Meno a priezvisko, rodné priezvisko, deň, mesiac, rok a miesto narodenia, štátne občianstvo, rodné číslo	Viktor Bejkovský 33-ročný neuvedené neuvedené neuvedené
Matka Meno a priezvisko, rodné priezvisko, deň, mesiac, rok a miesto narodenia, štátne občianstvo, rodné číslo	Gabriela Kendeová 34-ročná neuvedené neuvedené neuvedené
Poznámky	

v Rimavskej Sobote

dňa   31.5.   1996

Klára Csáková
meno a priezvisko matrikára

podpis

ŠEVT - 03 001 0   X/94/1   OAKOM Trebišov

Tomy's Birth Certificate

VILEM BEYKOVSKÝ 1867-1942

Vilem Beykovsky and František

1916

Marie Beykovsky b. Rosenbaum

Vilem Beykovsky

Marie Beykovsky

Vilem was born August 22, 1867 in Pitcovitz and died in the same place January 27, 1942. His grand-daughter Hanna Renee described how Vilem was scheduled to go to Terezin concentration camp, and he took his own life shortly before the pending departure with an overdose of pills. Vilem is buried in the Uhrineves cemetery, but there is no marker on his grave.

Vilem was a witness to my parent's wedding in Kocvar, Horovice, in the Czech Republic. Also Vilem was the advisor to my father, and they traveled together to lease the Sabatka Pusta, the farm in Slovakia, where my father worked and my family lived from 1930 to our departure to Ecuador in 1939.

Vilem died a tragic death. The local authorities informed Vilem that the property will be reverted to the new German government and he needed to vacate the premises. After Vilem announced to his wife that he decided to die, she called the family doctor to intercede; the doctor counseled Vilem, but to no avail. According to Hanna Fuchs, his grand daughter, Vilem went to bed in the evening and never woke up again.

I visited in 1995 with Mr. Tingel, who was a farm hand as a youngster at the Beykovský farm, told me that Vilem's wife mentioned Vilem taking an overdose of pills before he died. His death certificate show he died of congestive heart failure.

VILEM

MARIE ROSENBAUM 1880-1942

The Rosenbaum family lived in Pitkovitz and owned a paper pulp factory that produced mostly paper cups. Marie was born September 11, 1880, in Uvaly.

VILEM AND MARIE 1939

Marie married Vilem in Prague February 12, 1900, and they had one daughter and two sons (Anna, Frantisek and Jenik). Their mother Marie was taken to Terezin concentration camp on transport train the day after her birthday, September 12, 1942; then on October 8, 1942, she was transported to Treblinka and never seen again. Marie and her two sons were transported to Terezin together.

ANNA BEYKOVSKÝ 1902-1944

Anna was born on January 30, 1902, in Pitcovitz. Anna's mother was Marie and father was Vilem. She married Mudr. Adolf Elsner and they had one child: Hanna Renee born on January 26, 1926, in Prague.

Hanna and her father Adolf survived Terezin but Anna was taken to Auschwitz on October 6, 1944, where she perished.

I searched for descendants of this family for over four years, and finally in 2001, I located Hanna Fuchs, who was Vilem and Marie Beykovský's granddaughter. I had advertised in a German periodical dedicated to survivors of the Holocaust, and six months later I located Hanna. I was grateful that Hanna and her son Michael came to visit me in Everett, Washington, for my 70th Birthday.

TOM, HANNA AND GEORGE 2001

ANNA'S HUSBAND ADOLF ELSNER'S BIRTH CERTIFICATE

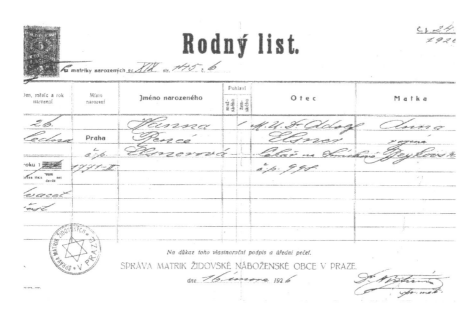

HANNA'S BIRTH CERTIFICATE

FRANTISEK BEYKOVSKÝ 1916-1942

Frantisek was born April 10, 1916, in Pitcovitz, AHE. Both
Frantisek and his brother Jenik were taken to the concentration camp,

ÚSTŘEDNÍ KARTOTÉKA — TRANSPORTY.

R. č. 51321

B e y k o v s k ý Hanuš

Rodná data: 22.12. 1918

Adresa před deportaci: Pitkovice č. 5 u Říčan

1. transport	2. transport
dne :	dne : 8.10.1942
	číslo : B U - 302
č. 529	do : Treblinky

TŘEDNÍ KARTOTÉKA — TRANSPORTY.

.32

B e y k o v s k ý František

ata: 10.4.1916

řed Pitkovice č. 5 u Říčan

1. transport	2. transport
	dne : 8.10.1942
	číslo : B U - 300
č. 527	do : Treblinky

TRANSPORT TO THE CONCENTRATION CAMP

230

FRANTISEK AND JENIK (HANUS). SEE H AND F.

accompanied by their mother Marie, by transport on September 12, 1942; then again on October 8, 1942 where they were murdered.

JENIK JIRI BEYKOVSKÝ 1918-1942

Jenik (Hanus) was born December 22, 1918 in Pitcovitz, CZ. Both Jenik and his brother Frantisek were taken to the Nazi concentration camp accompanied by their mother Marie by transport on September 12, 1942; then on October 8, 1942 where they were murdered.

DOCTOR OTTO BEYKOVSKÝ 1870-1935

Dr. Otto Beykovsky

Otto received a Doctor's degree in law from the University in Prague. In 1911, he passed his attorney exam. In 1922 his title was "Superior Financial Councilor" and he held the title until he retired in 1934. He died of stomach cancer one year later, on March 12, 1935, at the age of 64½.

Otto's tombstone exists at the Olsanske Hrbitovi, Jewish Cemetery in Prague, and has a black marble-tombstone with the locator number 5-11-32. On my trip to Prague with my brother Tom we found the tombstone flat on the ground covered mostly by ivy. We hired a cemetery worker and three days later we found the tombstone clean and erect and of course readable.

OTTO'S TOMBSTONE

The inscription on the face of the tombstone reads:
'HIGH FINANCIAL OFFICE STAFF' Dr. Jurisprudence Otto
Beykowsky born September 22, 1870 in Pitcovitz and died (Tuesday)
March 12, 1935 in Prague.
The inscription in Hebrew reads: *Here is buried our honored teacher,
Rabbi Issachar (may peace rest upon him) the son of the deceased
Josef Beykovský.*

HERMINA KRAUS 1875-1943

Hermina was born December 26, 1875, in Ksely, Cesky Brod about 25 miles east of Prague, and married Otto on April 7, 1918 in Prague. She was the daughter of Bernard Kraus and Francisca Stern. Hermina was deported on Transport AAr to Terezin June 16, 1942 and December 18, 1943 to Auschwitz on Transport Ds (with her son)

POLICE REGISTRATION FOR HERMINA

where they were murdered. She died a week short of her 68th birthday.

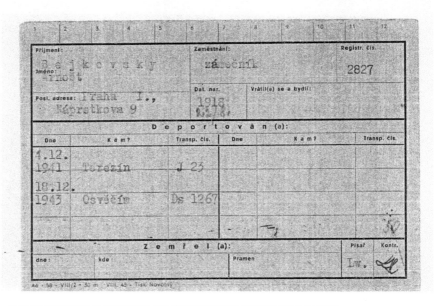

TRANSPORT CARDS FOR HERMINA AND ARGOTS TO THE CONCENTRATION CAMP

ARNOST (ERNST FRIEDRICH) BEYKOVSKÝ 1918-1943

Arnost was born on August 22, 1918, just four months after his

POLICE REGISTRATION FOR ARNOT

parent's marriage, in Prague, to parents Otto and Hermina. He was deported December 4, 1941, on Transport J to Terezin camp and December 18, 1943, sent to Auschwitz on Transport Ds where he was murdered. He barely lived four months after he turned 25 years old.

ANNA BEYKOVSKÝ 1875-1951

The youngest of four siblings, Anna was born September 15, 1875, in Pitcovitz and died January 28, 1951, in New Rochelle, New York. Dr. Viktor Pick was born February 5, 1871, and married Anna on September 19, 1897, in the Synagogue, a suburb of Prague named Königlish Weinbergen (Vinohrady). This is near where Louise and Josef Beykovský lived. Five generations of descendants from Viktor

VIKTOR AND ANNA - 1897

and Anna are still alive and living in USA.

New York State Department of Health
DIVISION OF VITAL STATISTICS
CERTIFICATE OF DEATH

Dist. No. 5904
To be inserted by registrar
Registered No. 54
6333

FOR GENEALOGICAL RESEARCH ONLY

IGNAZ AND EMMY KENDE

IGNAZ KENDE'S TOMBSTONE

TIKO MY GREAT GRANDSON

GRANDDAUGHTER ALYSSA AND LEO

CHAPTER 5

Rosa's Cookbook

The recipe notes are hand written in ink on onionskin paper in German, and later added inscriptions that link us as family; cover page reads: "Cookbook to Madame Louise Beykovský in Pitcovitz from Rosa Pollak; dated Pitcovitz 16 September 1875." By the way, Ana, Louise's daughter was born September 15, 1875 and the cookbook was dated next day.

Second Page at top: "Given as dowry to Ana Beykovský, Pitcovitz September 20, 1882. L.B."

Kochbuch

der

Madame *Louise* Beykowsky

aus *Pilkowitz*

zu

[signature]

Wildmitz 16./9ber 87...

The Cookbook of

Madame Louise (Dubsky)

Beykovsk

This cookbook is written in Pitkovitze,

From Rosa (Beykovský) Pollak Bistritz, September 16, 1875

This cookbook now belongs to my daughter

Ana Beykovský as an heirloom.

Pitkovitze. April 20, 1882

L.B.

Almond Torte

Take 3/4 lb. almonds, wipe them clean and grate them unpeeled, take 1 lb. sugar and crush it finely, mix it together, take 12 whole eggs, 8 yolks have to go in one after the other; 1/2 sp. cinnamon cup, a.1/2 cloves, rind of one lemon cut fine, 8 Tbs. blanched and chopped almonds, a. 1/4lb. grated bread without seeds, and you have to beat the dough together in one direction for one hour and then add spices and bread. Then grease a form and bake ----a chocolate icing over it and decorate it any way you want.

Sponge cake: Use 8 egg yolks, 2 whole eggs should be stirred together with 1/2 lb. granulated sugar until it is creamy; then take 12 tbsp flour, 1/4 lb. blanched and chopped almonds and mix it all very well together. Slowly add the 8 beaten egg whites and bake.

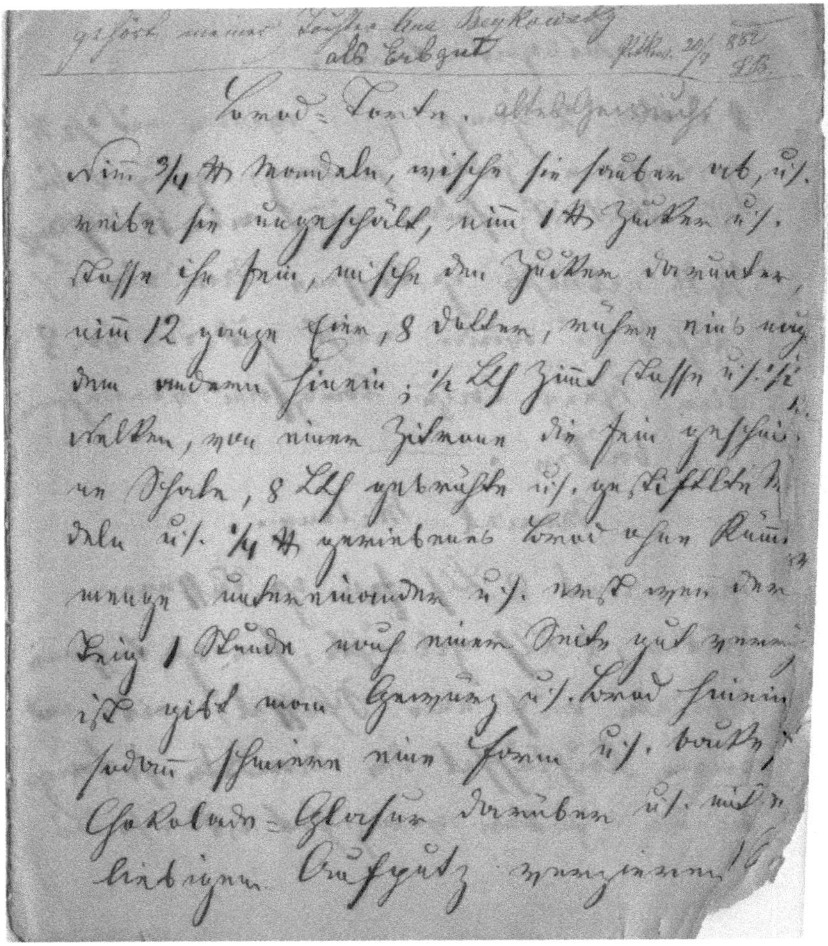

250

Mandel-Torte.

12 Lth fein gestoßenen Zucker welchen
früher an einer kleinen ganzen oder
großen halben Zitronen abgerieben wurde
12 Lth getrocknete gestoßenen oder geriebenen
Mandeln mit den abgeriebenen Zitronen
den Saft (zuletzt) 9 rohe Dotter lange
gerieben, zu allerletzt den Schnee
von 9 Eiweiß hinein langsam gemischt
u. backen. — Ein Zitronenglasur
bereiten von 1 Eiweiß, 6 Lth geriebenen
durchsiebten Zucker u. von 1/2 Limonie
den Saft hinein, u. dies zusammen 1 [illegible]
nach einer Seite gerührt. —

Almond Torte

12 Tbsp finely pounded sugar which was rubbed before; a whole small, or a large half grated lemon; 12 tsp soaked and pounded or grated almonds; the juice of the grated lemon; (lastly) 9 raw yolks slowly mixed in and at the very last 9 beaten egg whites to be added slowly and baked. A lemon icing over it of 1 egg white, 6 tsp grated and sifted sugar; the juice of 1/2 lemon, and all of this mixed together

Almond Melon

Take 8 tbsp. finely ground sugar, 8 tbsp blanched, finely chopped almonds and put them in a bowl. Grate together with a ladle until the sugar is completely dissolved and the almonds are starting to get wet, then take 8 egg yolks, add them one after the other and mix it very well, then take the beaten whites of 6 eggs and add it slowly and bake it nicely, but you can also cook it over steam first and then bake it - whatever you want.

Cinnamon Torte

Take1/2 lb finely chopped sugar, blanched and finely chopped almonds, 15 egg yolks, 1 whole egg, little lemon juice, 2 tsp cinnamon mix everything together well and bake it.

Nut? Cook (Roux)? 1/2 lb. nuts are shelled and the almonds grated fine, then 4 tsp butter, has to be worked over well, 8 egg yolks, one after the other mixed in, 8 tsp sugar finely chopped and lastly beaten whites of 6 eggs; grease the form well with butter, sprinkle with bread crumbs, the roux has to be cooked over steam for 3/4 hour; when you serve it, you have to put a chaudeau over it; you take 1/4 "Seidl" (Austrian liquid measure for beverages) liqueur, 1/4 "Seidl" cognac, 4 tsp sugar, 5 egg yolks and treat it like any Chaudeau (is a foamy wine sauce, made over steam).

Leibzelt = Torte.

8 Dotter, 2 ganze Eier, rühre mit ½ ℔
zerlassenem Zucker so lange gerühret bis
es dick ist; sodann nimm neben 12 Loth Mehl
¼ ℔ gebrühte zerlassene Mandeln u. s.
mische es wieder recht gut, der von 8
Eier Schnee dazu langsam vermischen
u. f. zellen. ————

Mandel Malaun.

Man nimmt 8 Loth fein zerlassenen
Zucker, 8 Loth gebrühte, fein zerlassene
Mandeln noch wie ein Schüssel, reibe mit
einem Reiblöffel die Mandeln so lange
bis der Zucker vermischt ist u. s. die

Paprika Fish

You take a lot of chopped onions, sauté them in a little piece of butter, then add the fish with a lot of paprika and a little water until the fish has simmered for quite a while (for 3 lbs. fish about 1/2 "Seidl" water,) then dissolve a thick, sweet (better if lightly sour) and pour it on the fish and let it simmer for a good while longer, dust with flour until it comes to another boil until the sauce is creamy and serve.

Anchovy/ Pike - Excellent

Anchovies should be washed and de-boned, and mix very well together with fresh butter cover the "slices" and let it bake.

Anchovy ----?

For 5 lbs. fish you have to take 1 lb. fresh butter and 1/8 lb. anchovies, finely mashed, cover and boil all this together, adding water often (1/4 Seidl), add a lot of chopped parsley and let it simmer for a while longer so that a little brown sauce can form.

Nuß-Reis.

½ ℔ Butter ... ...

... Butter ... ... , 8 Vollen
... ... , 8 Loth
Zucker ... ... zuletzt ... 6 ...
... ; die ... sind mit Butter ...
... , mit ... ...
... mit ¾ Stunden ...
... zur ... ...
... Chau d'eau ... ; ... ¼ ...
... , 4 Loth Zucker, 5 ... ...
... sich so ... ... Chau d'eau.

Chapter 6

The Land Registry in 1653

THE BEYKOVSKÝ'S LAND REGISTRY TRANSLATION

"Stavení rozbořených a pustých židovských, kdež toliko místa zůstávají

Jewish houses (in sense of estates-farms) ruined and empty, where sites are left only

Benessowský [Benešovský], Beykowsky [Bejkovský], Witowsky [Vítovský],

Enochowsky [Enochovský], Eliassowsky [Eliášovský], Markowsky,

školy židovský" is jewish schools.

The combination and order of words in the sentence is archaic-poetic - like from early years of 20th century or before. There is very handy fast Czech web dictionary on the internet - it could help you, it even have part sound, when you click on little speaker. It translates between few languages. Good luck. Jan Liska. http://slovnik.seznam.cz/

Luckily, Peter Zimmer had a copy of the article (attached). On page 15 (in Czech) and on page 49 (in German) the name BEYKOWSKY is mentioned. By a strange coincidence it relates to Turnov, which I presume is the same place that you visited.

Stadt Turnau (Turnov)
"Eingefallene und öde Judenhäuser, in denen nur hausen
Benessowský, Beykowsky, Witowsky, Enochowsky, Eliassowsky,
Markowsky,
Judenschulen"
Maybe this translates as:
"Fallen in and deserted Jewish houses, in which are only housed
Benessowský, Beykowsky, Witowsky, Enochowsky, Eliassowsky,
Markowsky,
Jewish schools".
It would be interesting to know how the the Czech version translates:
"Stavení rozbořených a pustých židovských, kdež toliko místa zůstávají

Benessowský [Benešovský], Beykowsky [Bejkovský], Witowsky [Vítovský], Enochowsky [Enochovský], Eliassowsky [Eliášovský], Markowsky, školy židovský"

I take it to mean that around 1653 a Beykowsky family was living in Turnau. Could this be the origins of the family in Schwenda ???

Regards, Peter

STUDIES AND ARTICLES

Lenka Matušíková

DIE JUDEN IM ERSTEN BÖHMISCHEN KATASTER 1653–1655*)

Die verheerenden Folgen des Dreißigjährigen Kriegs zeigten sich in Böhmen unter anderem auch durch ein stark angeschlagenes System der Steuereintreibung. Die Rechtsbefugnis des böhmischen Adels, auf dem Landtag die Höhe der geforderten Landessteuer gut zu heißen, diese auf die Anwesen der Untertanen umzulegen und einzutreiben, war im Verlauf der langen kriegerischen Auseinandersetzung faktisch auf die Beamten der Hofkammer übergegangen. Diese suchten den Finanzbedarf des Staates vor allem durch Anhebung der alten Verbrauchssteuern (z. B. Tranksteuer) sowie durch Einführung neuer Verbrauchssteuern zu decken. Nach Kriegsende suchten die Böhmischen Landstände ihre Vorrechte wieder zu erlangen und forderten daher auf dem am 4. Dezember 1652 abgehaltenen Landtag vom Herrscher, dass letztmalig 1652 die Steuern von dessen Beamten eingetrieben werden sollten und dass die Verbrauchssteuern von einer Grundsteuer, d.h. von der Besteuerung der Untertanenanwesen abgelöst werden sollte. Die Hofkammer wehrte sich gegen ein solches Ansinnen mit der Behauptung, die Steuereinnahme aus den Untertanenanwesen erreiche die erforderliche Höhe nicht, da die Obrigkeiten in ihren "Bekenntnisbriefen" oder "Einbekenntnissen", also den Steuerklärungen jener Zeit, nicht die wahre Anzahl ihrer Hintersassen und Leibeigenen angäben und die Zahl der Anwesen im Land unbekannt sei. Ferdinand III. stimmte schließlich zu, dass die Steuer künftig wieder von den ständischen Einnehmern eingetrieben werden sollte, vorausgesetzt, dass diese deren ordnungsgemäße Einziehung und rechtzeitige Abführung in der vom Landtag festgesetzten Höhe gewährleisteten. Dieser setzte fest, dass die Steuerpflicht alle Güter in Böhmen beträfe mit Ausnahme derer, die als verödet neu besiedelt wurden und deren Wirte durch den Landtagsbeschluss von 1650 für drei Jahre von der Steuer befreit waren. Die vom Herrscher geforderte Summe von 200 000 Gulden sollte so beigetrieben werden, dass daran sowohl Untertanen als auch deren Obrigkeiten, Bergbau- und königliche Städte, Gespansthöfe, Freisassen, Schulzen, Inleute, Kaufleute, Schäfermeister und -knechte und nicht zuletzt auch Juden teilhaben sollten. Diesen wurde auferlegt, für jeden erwachsenen Mann über 20 Jahren 4 Gulden 40 Kreuzer zu entrichten und für jeden Knaben im Alter von 10 bis 20 Jahren (über 10 Jahren) 2 Gulden 20 Kreuzer.[1]

*) Diese Arbeit entstand im Rahmen des vom Institut für Geschichte der Juden in Österreich, St. Pölten, unterstützten Projektes "Bohemia, Moravia et Silesia Judaica."
1) Näher zur gesamten Problematik vergl. Josef Pekař: *České katastry 1654–1789* [Böhmische Kataster 1654–1789], Praha 1932, S.4ff. T. A. Slavík: O popisu Čech po třicetileté válce. *Zprávy Zemského archivu království Českého*, III, Praha 1910, S.24 (T. A. Slavík: Böhmens Beschreibung nach dem 30jährigen Kriege, *Mitteilungen aus dem Landesarchive des Königreiches Böhmen*, Bd. III, Praha 1910, S.29 ff); Karel Doskočil: *K edici berní ruly, Berní rula 1 (Úvodní pojednání)* [Zur Edition der Steuerrolle, Steuerrolle 1 (Einleitende Abhandlung)], Praha 1950, S.35ff.

5

265

CHAPTER 7

Correspondence from the Rezek's

Dear George,

We are sorry to be so long in answering your letter, but we have just returned from Toronto where unfortunately Joe's Mother died. She was a wonderful lady of nearly 98 years.

I do have some pictures of Josef Beykosvsky and also pictures of Hana (his daughter, I think) and her grandson Mathieu. Hana was taught by Joe's cousin Helena until she was sent to Thereisin and then Auschwitz. I also have 2 booklets to send you. I do not know which one you refer to when you speak about Hugo Gold? One is a little pamphlet and the other is a small booklet about the Jews of Uhrineves until 1942 when all were deported.

I have copies of other pamphlets which may interest you and will copy and send. Please be patient as we are both Jet lagged and I have to get organised. I will also send copies of the Uhrineves Archives and of the Jewish community there from the mid 1980"s. If you have not got it. Have you got Hana's address in Prague? Libuse has it. Maybe she has an E. Mail. Have you been in contact with a David Rose in London ? he and his synagogue adopted the town of Uhrineves and the Sefer torah of the shule.

If your G Grandfather is buried in the cemetery in Uhrineves , next time we visit I will try and get a snap shot for you. Do you remember visiting Uhrineves before you left? Maybe you remember some of the Rezek family at that time. Perhaps later we can compare our family trees and history. Luckily there are many of our descendants in Israel and in Canada.

Please keep in touch , It was good to hear from you.

Avery and Joe Rezek

xxx

From: "George Beykovský" <Beykovský@verizon.net>To: <joer@netvision.net.il>
Sent: Friday, August 08, 2008 10:04 AM
Subject: Uhrineves

I heard much about your family from Libuse. I am descendant of Josef Beykovský. He is my g-g-father. His son is Gustav and my father Viktor. I was born in Slovakia and left home in 1939-luckily. Do you have any photographs to share of the Beykovský? I have copies of Hugo Gold's book.

Chapter 8

Letter From Hans to Gracie

October 8, 1971

My Dearest Gracie:
Before I continue with my story with my father's side of the family, I want to tell two episodes concerning my grandparents Lichtenstadt. About 70 years ago, my grandfather took me on a hike starting in the Styrian village of Tragöb, a charming spot at the bottom of the Hochschwab Mountain. Grandfather hired a guide, equipped with a wooden torch, soaked in pitch, for a passage through the Frauenmauer cavern. It took quite a long time, maybe an hour, some stretches were quite narrow, but there was no real difficulty. It looked quite eerie by flickering light of the torch. We finally emerged on the other side of the mountain and descended to the mining town of Eisenerz. Maybe mining is not the right word -on the Erzberg; iron ore is being won from the surface, like on the exhausted Mesabi Range in America. This experience made such an impression on me that I did not forget it after all these years, although I do not remember anymore quite a number of much more spectacular hikes.
During the war (WWI, of course,) my sister Mimi — she was about 23 or 24 at the time — left the family home. Or was it shortly after the war? She took her own room near the slopes of the Vienna woods. At that time, Vienna was hungry, there was hardly any food to be bought and my older friends keep telling me how they suffered during these years. (I was not very sympathetic, because in Siberia, where I was at the time, the food shortage was even worse.) My

269

grandparents were lucky, because grandfather was manager of the restaurant chain of the Suppen- and Teeanstalt and so had an opportunity to provide some extra rations for his family. Now grandmother was quite concerned about Mimi, the child could starve for all she knew. So she took a basket of food to Mimi's place while Mimi was at work in the Länderbank. She left the supplies with the landlady who wanted to know who she was. Grandmother gave the name of Mrs. Brzezina, hut she did not fool Mimi who immediately guessed her right identity.

I never knew the parents of my father. They were Jacob and Rosa Pollak, nëe Beykowsky, and lived in Bistritz in Bohemia, now CSSR. They had a large farm there and lived on the town square. And they had eight children of whom I knew only six. My father was the seventh child. One of the older children was aunt Berta, married to Alfred Gärtner. I mentioned her before her sister-in-law was Tante Emma blond, aunt of my mother. Aunt Berta and uncle Alfred lived in Svijan-Podol, Bohemia (CSSR), where uncle Alfred was a tenant farmer on a large scale. They used to send us a barrel of apples and a barrel of pears every fall, so the poor relatives would have some fruit. It was most welcome.

In the summer of 1910 I visited with them in their mansion-like home. It must have been an ancient castle. Of their eight children, all of whom I knew, only two girls were at home at the time, about 2 and 3 years older than me. They were both healthy specimens, educated, and a little mischievous. I courted both of them specially Hedda, a real beauty, taller than I, and a splendid figure. Your mother met her in 1938 in Prague when Hedda, married to a jeweler named Epstein, was about 47 years old. Your mother considered her still beautiful. We embraced and kissed like it were only a short time since our last encounter in 1910. Uncle Alfred and Aunt Emma blond, his sister, were the first relatives I met on my return from Siberia. They visited me in a quarantine camp in Pardubice, not too far distant from Svijan, before I was discharged.

Oldest child was Vally. She studied in Vienna and was in frequent touch with our family, as were most of my many cousins of *both sexes. Of her eight children, two boys, veritable giants, survived concentration camp and immigrated to Canada, where their uncle Gustl lived in Peter's Corner - I mentioned him before. Second was Vilos, a never-do-well who was mostly supported by his parents and brothers. Vilos resembled my father so much that people who knew my father believed he was his son. Richard was a typical Gärtner who looked very much like Paul Lichtentstadt, the some of Emma blond, the nee Gärtner.*

Richard was a successful engineer. Next was Gustav, he became a farmer who raised all farm products imaginable except chicken. In Canada, he became a chicken farmer. He is an artist, a painter and decorator who did most of the work in his beautiful big house. He is now retired and we exchange Christmas messages every year. He and Oily, the chicken-sexer (she examines newly hatched chickens and determines their sex which determines their future handling), and have a daughter who is married to an atomic scientists and lives with him somewhere in the wilderness. She has a Ph.D. in botany. Gustav and Oily were always very kind and "family-like" whenever I happened to drop in on them. They also came to New York once and stayed at an elegant hotel, but I think, they preferred Peter's Corner.

I have mentioned Hedda who came next, after her came Ada. I am not quite sure about her life. She married a Mr. Stern and lived in Bruno, underground during the Nazi occupation. I had no contact with her and heard only, probably from Gustav, that she died some time ago. Last were the identical twins, Eugene and Eric. Your mother met Eugene while on a Mediterranean cruise in 1936. (I had so many relatives she could not help to know one or the other.) When we made out the list of our wedding announcements, we found out that we both listed Eugene Gärtner at the same Prague address. Eugene owned a coal store and was quite well to do. He had studied in Vienna and since we were not far apart in age, we became sort of playmates. Erich was a forwarder in Hamburg who took care of my move from Vienna to New York. Like all my Czech relatives, he paid no attention to my warnings that Czechoslovakia was obviously next on Hitler's line of conquests. *His New York correspondent, Mr. Freedman of Freedman & Slater, offered to take him to the American consul in Amsterdam where they met in early 1939, who would issue him a visa immediately and to come to America right away, even without a penny. He knew him as a clever, experienced man who would certainly do well in America. Erich sent his wife and two boys to Davos, Switzerland, and stayed in Hamburg. There was so much business with all those Jews going to America! He was never heard from again.*

When I went to America in 1938, I had a stopover in Prague of two weeks. I saw most of the Gärtner there and pleaded with all of them, entreated them, warned them. Eugene took me for a ride to Vally Back who lived with her family on a farm about 30 mi. away. All were most kind, offered me help, which I did not need, but refused to see their own danger. They considered me sort of crazy - how can a man leave Europe for strange America! Besides, CSSR was not Austria, they had fortifications, they had allies, they would fight, and they would never surrender like the Austrians did. No, sir! And they were Czech patriots, reserve officers it never made any difference that they were Jews. And they were much too comfortable. They could not bear to leave their elegant homes, their rambling farms, their prosperous businesses, and make a new start. I felt like Cassandra. I was convinced of what fate had in store for them, but I could not make them believe me, all these people who had shown me much kindness and love were doomed and I knew it, hut could not save them.

Next in line after aunt Berta was uncle Emil whose picture I took in Prague in 1938 when he was about as old as I am now. He was one of my favorites. Gustl kept telling me, that I look like him. Well, we were both typical Pollak's. Uncle Emil took over the family farm in Bistritz where I was several times his guest as a little boy. Uncle Emil would take me along on. His inspection tour of his fields told us a lot about the grains and other things. I watched at milking time and saw the records kept of each, cow of how much milk they gave each day and how rich it was in fat. I watched the separator and the butter churn. I did not like so much the distillery that was attached to the farmhouse. The machinery scared me, while uncle Emil tried to explain to me the workings of a steam engine.

Evenings uncle Emil would play the flute and aunt Karla nee Fuchs, the piano.

Uncle Emil was the best storyteller I ever knew. I never got tired of his story of the crazened plum dumpling. And aunt Karla pampered me with her cooking. They did not have any children. They both loved music and would travel to Vienna to hear the opera or some symphony concert. They used to send us regularly 5 kilo packages of fresh country butter which was always most welcome. Uncle Emil would also take me on rides on a horse-drawn carriage to some neighbors, one of which was a brother, Leopold, called uncle Poldi. During the war uncle Emil, then about 50, felt he had worked long enough. He sold the farm and invested the purchase price in safe bonds, which assured him an adequate income. He moved to Prague, indulged in his hobbies to which he added photography. He knew practically everybody in Prague and was everywhere well liked and respected. But this enjoy- merit did not last long. Inflation made his bonds worthless and he was forced to go back to work. He became a salesman. By his personal contacts he was frequently able to clinch sales nobody else could. Or he would find scarce merchandise and the customer who needed it. And he was quite happy and made money, too.

When we went on our honeymoon in 1936 to Prague, aunt Karla was dying. She had two sisters. One of them, Ludmilla aunt Lidl was married to a hotel manager who wound up as manager of the two most elegant hotels in Vienna, the Bristol and the Imperial, the latter right next door to my present apartment. Aunt Marzenka was married to a manufacturer of paper twine, I forget his name. They came to New York and your mother met her. For the last time I saw uncle Emil in 1938. He was a sick man, hut still happy with his nurse who lived with him. I am afraid he liked her better than he did aunt Karla during the last years. Of course, he refused to leave Prague for America. He would not leave his place until lie would be carried-out feet first. I never heard from him again, I only hope he died before the Nazis caught up with him.

Uncle Leopold or rather Poldi came next. He had illusions of grandeur and called himself "Grobgrundbesitzer", while in fact he was usually in a financial pinch. He lived with his family in the village of Olbramovice, not far from Bistritz, in a rambling farmhouse with aunt Kamilla, nee Kohn, and five children one of whom you know, Else Kraus who died this year in Ramat Chen, Israel. Uncle Poldi was not nearly as clever and talented as uncle Emil and there was little reason for his conceit. Aunt Kamilla was a doll. Uncle Poldi died at about 50 during a stay in Vienna of a heart attack while visiting an establishment of poor reputation. On my return from Siberia, I stopped over for a while in Olbramovice. Aunt Camilla welcomed me like I was her own boy and I was immediately at home with her. I do not remember now which one of the cousins was at home at the time: whoever it was cared. It was an infinitely more cordial welcome than I got from my own family a few days later in Vienna. The oldest daughter was Hanna, about 3 years older than me. She had studied for some time in Vienna and we used to be on pretty good terms. She married Max Stern, an engineer. They had to struggle pretty hard during the first years of their marriage only lately they began to prosper. They had a bright, boy, George, a mountain climber and brilliant student. When I tried to warn them of the Hitler menace, they acted much like the Gärtner. Max was a respected member of the engineering society they would never turn on him on account of his Jewish faith. It was hopeless. Hella, the second daughter, was strikingly beautiful, raven-haired, tall and very intelligent. To the dismay of her parents, she became an enthusiastic, scientist and went off to Palestine to work in a Kibbutz. It was hard work and with time her enthusiasm waned. She returned to Czechoslovakia in the thirties and married a Mr. Bruml. Her happiness did not last long. The Bruml, too, would not listen to my warnings in 1938, more the pity. Mr. Bruml had a sister, Kathe Bruml, owner of the Ring-Buchhandlung in Vienna, across the Ringstrabe from the university. She came to America and worked as a domestic in New Rochelle. Your mother knew her.

Else, later Mrs. Kraus was next. She was about two years younger than I, she studied languages in Vienna for several years, notably English. Mrs. Kraus translated the Forsythe Saga (Galsworthy) from English into Czech or German I forget which. We got along famously she was one of my favorite cousins. She married Rudi Kraus, director of some factory. They lived very comfortably in a large apartment in Prague and had the sweetest children anybody can wish for, Dolly and Hans who both studied later in America and were a couple of times in our house. One of them stayed with us, I am not sure now which. As children they were models and simply charming. They were about 5 and 6 years old when we met them first in Prague in 1936. And when we came back to Prague in 1958, the Kraus were about to go on a trip. Else handed me the keys to their apartment and told us to make ourselves at home. The Kraus were the only ones to realize the coming danger; they went to Israel and were safe. One niece followed them, the daughter of Karl, youngest brother. Hanca, Hans was a fool and a show-off, in this respect a little like his father. He inherited the farm and mismanaged it he would never listen to the sound advice of uncle Emil. But he managed to marry rich, the daughter of a Vienna banker. He sold the farm and went to Prague to live. He was lucky he died young of natural causes.

Karl, the youngest, was a gangling fellow, good natured and sensible. He married the daughter of a neighboring farmer, also named Pollak, but no relation. He never came to Vienna, so I had contact with him only when I came to Olbramovice.

Aunt Klara was the one of my uncles and aunts I saw most of, because she lived in Vienna. She was married to Hans Schiller, an official of the state railroad. I remember him as a short gray-haired man with a well-trimmed turned-up moustache, always immaculate. They were the ones where all the cousins stayed when they came to Vienna to study. From 1901 to 1908 we lived very near their place. In fact, their apartment, on top of the Wilhelm bakery, was right, across the street Diesterweggasse, from the elementary school to which I went. Sometimes, I dropped in at Aunt Klara's after school. She always had some treat for me, which I appreciated. I shall never forget the day when she put before me a large tray with Buchteln; ask your mother for a definition. It was a Czech cake. You normally take one piece or two at most. I finished off the whole tray and aunt Klara watched without blinking or interfering. She probably baked another batch after I left.

Aunt Klara and uncle Hans were great musicians. Each season, they would produce a series of chamber music concerts at their modest home. Aunt Klara played the piano together with Mr. Roth, a well-known composer of the time, uncle Hans conducted, and the bassoon was attended by Prof. Madensky of the Philharmonic orchestra and the Opera. Even the participating amateurs were accomplished. The audience was small: my own family and the brother of uncle Hans, uncle Karl, with his daughter Anna (Antschi), a year older than me and an early playmate. Aunt Lili knew Anna Schiller well as the secretary of the Deutsches Volkstheater and respected her. In the evening was regularly topped with a huge dinner. Aunt Klara was also a pretty good chess player. She died in 1916.

Uncle Heinrich lived in Berlin where I visited him in the spring of 1914. I wanted to contact the German counterpart of our Vienna youth movement. His wife, Henriette, -aunt Hetty - was Aryan, a typical efficient German woman. They had a very pretty daughter, about 4 or 5 years younger than me who killed herself as a young girl, I don't know why. Uncle Heinrich, and aunt Hetty owned and managed the Frödbelin Institute on Wilhelmstrabe. Girls learned housekeeping there and served as maids in a hotel. Uncle Heinrich disagreed very much with my views, articles, and speeches, but we played happily chess together. I never knew what happened to him and aunt Hetty.

The most interesting of my uncles was uncle Otto, the youngest. He was a physician and during my early childhood he was a ship doctor with, the Loyd Triestino. He usually traveled to the orient and would bring souvenirs to all the family: swords in ivory scabbards, fans, vases, lacquered Chinese boxes and what have you.

All my uncles were tall, but also bulky, Otto was lean and the only blond. He tried very hard to find a cure for cancer. He later had a sanitarium in South Tyrol, which failed and the brothers had to bail him out. He was frequently in financial trouble and required help from the family and he was considered the black sheep. I liked him very much as he was different! Late in life he married a Baltic princess, divorced, with 8 children, Gertrude - aunt Trude. The oldest daughter, Gaby, was a dancer in Vienna. At one time, she met a playboy there, Paul Frankel, whom I knew from the Semmering. He plied her with drinks and then seduced her. When she became pregnant, she killed herself.

The last time I saw uncle Otto was in the last months of 1914. I got my basic training in the Felsenreitschule in Salzburg, now the scene of the Salzburg festivals. Uncle Otto had acquired another sanitarium in Parsch where he lived now with aunt Trude and one stepdaughter. It was a ghastly place, completely empty except for the three of them. And uncle Otto was dying. Water was rising through his legs into the abdomen; he knew very well that he was doomed. By now, there is a cure for his predicament, but at that time it was considered incurable.

I have to mention still another branch of the family. Anna Beykovský was a cousin of my father's on his mother's side — his mother was a nee Beykovský. She was married to Mr. Viktor Pick, a physician, and we saw them occasionally when they passed through Vienna. Their son was Eric Pick of Gaylordsville, Conn. whom you knew —he died this year. They also had a daughter Ada, married to Friedrich Berger, an insurance agent. Ada is a very talented designer of folklore dresses and lives in Manhattan., but she does not seem to care about the family, at least as far as we are concerned.

The hardest part for me (next to talking about myself) is to talk about my parents, your grandparents. All the relatives I have mentioned were respectable and likable people- my parents were not. My father, Hugo Pollak, was born in Bistritz on October 19, 1866, the year of the war between Austria and Prussia. (Austria Lost miserably) He became an accountant with the Länderbank in Vienna and married mother in 1892- I told you that before. Father had always illusions, mostly about himself. Before marriage, he had played the field, always with the cheapest type of girls, and contracted VD. I am afraid he never stopped and gave mother pretty good reason for her jealousy. I am sure about it in. his late years, he confided his experiences to me. My father thought of himself always as a potential manager and was terribly frustrated when one of his fellow accountants rose to the job as general manager. (He was a very bad one, Mr. Rotter, that is.) So the family finances were pretty poor until 1908 when father was named chief accountant of the Rumanian subsidiary in Bucharest. They had a large apartment in (Galea Academiei and had to entertain. Father filled the house with paintings and rugs, which he considered a shrewd investment, hut he did not have any real knowledge of art, it was a haphazard accumulation with not a single good piece in the lot. And father prided himself as an art connoisseur. He bought two second hand cars and hired a chauffeur-mechanic who was sometimes once in a week able to get one car going enough for a ride to the city park. And father and mother showed off in their miserable buggy. He finally sold the cars at a loss. His only interest besides women was cards. He used to play cards for hours in a coffeehouse with similar cronies. He also used to play cards with mother- they had no topic for conversation. They also used to play chess, and this is how I learned to play it myself, by watching them. There were always violent arguments between then at these games.

In 1910 my parents, sister and brother returned to Vienna. Father had a job there as chief accountant of a metal factory belonging to the Länderbank. We had a large apartment on the Donaukanal, between Urania and Schwedenbrücke, if you remember your Vienna. It was not a bad location. The apartment was crammed with paintings and rugs. Father would have it appear like a museum, it was more like a mess. And it was not comfortable to live in. He did never get along well with mother and so preferred to spend his evenings in his favorite coffeehouse playing cards. 1914 he had to join the army, he was a reserve-lieutenant and even was promoted during the war to Oberleutnant. He saw action in the Carpathian Mountains, but was mostly used in the supply section. At age 50, in Bartfa, he contracted syphilis, from which he suffered to his death. This was *before penicillin, you know. During the inflation of the early 20's, father made money through speculation. He had accumulated a. collection, of diamonds and it would have been. A shrewd idea to hold on. But he wanted to make a large profit and gave them to a "friend" to sell in Argentina. The "friend." was never heard from again. Father had retired early from the Länderbank - he felt, he was a rich man and did not need to work again. After the coup with the diamonds, he went back to work as a bank accountant. He sublet two rooms of the apartment. This was the situation when I returned from Siberia in August 1921. . By now, father was sorry; he had sublet the two rooms, one of them the largest in the apartment, because by the rent freeze the return did hardly matter. He could finally evict the tenants by claiming that my return required more room. My room was a very small one, my younger brother, George, got the large one. Father changed jobs a couple of times and retired eventually for good. He could live on his pension. He spent most of his time dozing, or he went to his coffeehouse to play cards. He had little contact with his brothers and sisters, except for aunt Klara, as long as she lived. He sort of felt it an injustice that they were all so much better off than himself, except for poor uncle Otto. He died miserably after a long illness of paralysis in a hospital - in a single room - in the spring of 1935.*

During vacation time we always went to the country, preferably the mountains. And I must be grateful that I learned this way to love the open scene and the mountains. I always left Vienna the day after school closed. If my parents were not ready to leave yet, they shipped me off to one or the other of the Bohemian uncles where I was always welcome. Father had only 4 weeks vacation, but mother and we children always spent two months in the country, mostly at a farmhouse where mother could do her own cooking. I remember one vacation that was different. About 1910, we went to Venice where we stayed at a cheap hotel in the middle of the city. Mornings we visited the galleries and churches - I fell in love with, a Madonna by the older Bellini in a church near the, Riva degli Schiavoni and the afternoons were spent at the Lido. I can still remember how shocked my mother

279

was at the sign of the first one-piece bathing suit, which immediately became the cynosure of the whole male crowd.

The summer of 1909 was spent in Rosenau in Burzenland, then part of Southern Hungary, now of Rumania. We collected more mushrooms there than mother could cut up and dry. From Rosenau, we went on a hike of the Buczecz (pr. Bootshetsh). It started with a buggy ride to the foot of the mountain, where father hired a guide. We slept in a mountain cabin and reached the summit (ca. 2200m) the next morning. It was the highest mountain I had climbed so far. I never dreamed that seven years later I was to camp there on a ridge opposite Buczecz in winter during the war.

The summers of 1912 and 1913 were spent in Veldes, Krain, now Bled, Jugoslavia. This was a most beautiful place on a warm little lake with an island in its middle and a little church on the island. A castle was situated on top of a precipice leading right into the lake. And to the north were the Karawanken mountains and to the east the Julian Alps. My parents, Mimi and Schorschi mostly went swimming or on short promenades around. By that time I was 18 and 19 and I started out for myself into the mountains. I traversed the whole Karawanken range in two days and used to climb the Hochstuhl, highest in the Karawanken. In record time.

But my most memorable climb was that of legendary Triglav, 2800m, top of the Julian Alps. I had to take a short train ride to Lengenfeld, I think, on which I met a young girl who looked like she wanted to go on a hike. I invited her to join me and she agreed. I started up the Urata Valley at. A furious pace and we were in a couple of hours at the Aljaz cabin and the foot. of the forbidding north wall of the Triglav. The girl thought this was fine; we had lunch there and could return now. But that was not my idea. I knew there was a trail with ladders and fixed ropes, the Tominsek put, up to the Triglav plateau. She was a good sport and came along. We reached a cabin of the Slovenian Alpine Club where we spent the night in separate dormitories. The next morning we climbed the summit with the help of more ladders and ropes - my highest mountain, at that time. For the descent I had chosen a very long trail through the romantic Seven

Lakes Valley. Funny thing, I had no other use for the girl than as a hiking companion. We were the only hikers for miles around but it never occurred to me to take advantage of the situation. The Valley ended in the Komarcza Wall and a steep trail led down to the Savitza falls, a large cascade. The girl kept up with my pace and never wavered. We than had to march past long Wocheiner Lake to the railway station of Wocheiner Feistritz in time for a train that took me back to Veldes and her to I don't know where. I never heard from her again.

In 1913, uncle William Kreitner joined us in Veldes. He was the widower after father's oldest sister, Luise, whom I never knew. He was a well-to-do retired merchant and lonely. He wanted to make a trip to the Dolomites of South Tyrol and wanted me to come along. Poor uncle Willy! He never guessed what was in store for him. I did not take him up high mountains, but the hikes across passes and the like were about as much as he could take and he would never have gone to all that trouble without me. But I got him really up to the Bamberger cabin on Fedaja Pass right at the foot of the glacier-coated Marmolata, 3340m. I wheedled him into agreeing to let me climb Marmolata while he stayed at the cabin. He almost died from fear I would kill myself while I had the time of my life climbing a real mountain. Uncle Willy never forgot this Dolomite trip. In his memory he had climbed Marmolata himself, I am afraid.

I hate to talk about my mother even more than I do about my father. Father was weak, but mother was mean. She was born Thekla Lichtenstadt in Vienna on September 4, 1871 - almost exactly 100 years ago. She married early 1892, and was soon dissatisfied with married life, especially the modest means of my father at the time. She envied her sisters who lived with grandfather and shared a much more interesting and comparatively abundant life. She envied most poor aunt Selma who deserved more to be pitied; her life was a string of tragedies against which her wealth was no remedy.

I learned to hate mother early in life, when she forced food down my throat, when she hurt me when combing my hair or cutting my fingernails. Like all kids, I was a little devil and she beat me,

*frequently for no other reason than her mean temper. She would revile
me by using profane invectives, they were her daily language, also
towards my father, When I got anything but all A's in school, I was
punished severely. I do not know exactly what education mother had.
She was quite good at English and French and a voracious reader. In
the earlier years of her married life, she used to accompany father on
bicycle trips – that was the only active sport I know of, aside from
swimming, she ever performed.*

*She hated housework and always had a maid, even during the
lean years. Whenever she was without one for a while, she was in a
constant fit. She treated her maids very badly and made them work
from morning till late at night. Worst part was that she was most
inconsiderate. She would ring for the maid when she was most busy
and then keep her waiting for her order until she had finished the
chapter of her novel she was just reading. Poor disfigured old Mary
had to sleep in a folding iron cot in the kitchen, which she had to set
up each night and put away each morning. She was stingy, maybe a
habit formed during the time when they were poor. I hated to beg for
every penny I needed and have to argue about it before she gave me
reluctantly what I needed. So I started tutoring when I was 15, so I
won't have to ask her for money. And she had lovers - well, father was
not faithful either - I only knew of two of them who were the most
obvious ones, I was not really interested to find out whatever she did
in the absence of father during the war. The worst time in our family,
were the meals. Father had the bad habit of criticizing the cooking
which made her furious to the point she would hit father. Or he would
suggest she leave the maid a larger helping. That was even worse. "So
you care more about the bitch than you do about me!" was one of her
favorite arguments. One evening meal probably around 1930 I shall
never forget. At that time I worked in the bank without time out for
lunch, so I developed a healthy appetite for dinner, my only big meal
of the day. One evening, we had Mimi's family as guests for dinner.
Dinner dragged a little in preparation and I may have shown some
sign of impatience. When it was finally served, mother gave me my
plate, saying "Da frib!" You say that to a dog. I rose without a word*

and went to a restaurant for my dinner. After dinner I returned as if nothing had happened.

When I returned from Siberia after seven years of absence, interrupted only by a short leave 5 years earlier, I had notified my parents of the date of my arrival in Vienna. When I rang the bell of our apartment old Mary opened and recognized me immediately. Nobody was home. Nothing had been done to clear up the mess accumulated in my old room. I felt like returning to Siberia!

In 1938, it was already clear that I would go to America and I would take care of arrangements for America for the other members of the family except for mother who was ill and not expected to live long anyway. I am sure, Schorschi could have done very well in America, much better than me. The daily life with mother was mostly responsible for his weakness that made him kill himself. Worst part was that Mimi refused to leave Europe as long as mother lived. She finally died in April, 1939, and Mimi and Ernst made it by the skin of their teeth - and my efforts to Norway a few days before the start of the war and from there to America the day before Hitler invaded Norway.

Well, Gracie, that's about where you come from.

Love and kisses.

Note: Harry Polk was born Hans Gunter Pollak on May 3, 1894, and died August 24, 1983.

Gracie and George in New York

Appendix A

Family Trees

JANUARY 2006 - DESCENDANTS OF JACOB DUBSKY

1 Jacob Dubsky 1760 -
+Rosalia Dubsky 1760 -
2 Salomon Dubsky 1788 - 1856
+Anna Stern 1786 - 1849
 3 Elias Dubsky 1809 -
 3 Pinkas Josef Dubsky 1811 -
 3 Horsch Dubsky 1813 -
 3 Abraham Dubsky 1815 -
 +Francisca (Nany) Schmolka 1823 - 1897
  4 Louise Dubsky 1843 - 1909
  +Josef Beykovský 1834 - 1921
   5 Gustav Beykovský 1864 –

Grandfather of George B.

   +Luise Glück 1867 - 1929
   5 Vilem Beykovský 1867 - 1942
   +Marie Sara Rosenbaum 1880 - 1942
   5 Otto Beykovský 1870 - 1935
   +Hermine Kraus 1875 - 1943
   5 Anna Beykovský 1875 - 1951
   +Viktor Dr. Pick 1871 -
  4 Moritz Dubsky 1845 -
  4 Wilhelmine Dubsky 1846 – 1925

Ancestors of Erich Lewitus

  +Josef Dr. Pick 1830 -
   5 Karel Phil Bedrich Pick 1875 -
   5 Friedrich Carl Bedrich Pick 1875 -

1943

   +Paula Hellin 1880 -
   5 Rudolfine Pick 1877 - 1930
   +Dr. Otto Heller 1868 - 1943
  4 Eduard Dubsky 1848 -
  4 Anna Dubsky 1850 -
  +N. Stern
   5 Marie Stern 1880 -
  4 Sofie Dubsky 1853 -
  +N.Klein 1850 -
  4 Ludvik Dubsky 1855 -
  4 Frederika Dubsky 1858 -
  +N. Freiberger 1847 -
   5 Rudolf Dr.Ing Freiberger 1906 -
  4 Sallomon Otto Dubsky 1860 -
  4 Julie Elisabetha Dubsky 1862 -
  4 Josefa Dubsky 1864 -

        4   Hugo Dubsky   1866 - 1942
3   Bernard Dubsky   1827 - 1890
        +Eleonora Fürth   1839 - 1932
        4   Salomon Dubsky 1856 - 1942

DESCENDANTS OF ADOLF BEYKOVSKÝ

```
1     Adolf Beykovský 1833 - 1871
..   +Rosalie Fischel
.... 2   Kamilla Beykovský   1859 - 1937
........          +Leopold Jerusalem   1849 - 1926
.......... 3        Ida Jerusalem  1879 - 1940
.............          +Emil Frank   - 1929
.......... 3        Margarethe Jerusalem 1881 - 1934
.............          +Alfred Schick        1872 - 1927
.......... 3        Therese Jerusalem     1883 - 1942
.............          +Otto Hellman        1868 - 1929
.......... 3        Alice Jerusalem        1886 - 1888
.......... 3        Gabriele Jerusalem     1888 - 1942
.............          +Gustav Adler 1877 - 1942
.... 2   Ludmila Beykovský   1861 - 1934
........          +Friedrich Schulhof   -1902
.......... 3        Rudi Schulhof 1889-
.......... 3        Rosl Schulhof  1882
.............          +Martos
.......... 3        Ida Schulhof    1882 - 1941
.............          +Karl Rosenzweig      1871-1941
.......... 3        Otto Schulhof 1878 – 1942
                     + Elsa  1882 - 1942
.... 2   Emil Beykovský        1863 -
.... 2   Julius Beykovský      1864 – 1942
                     + Josefa Friedmann 1872-1942
.......... 3        Adolf Beykovský      1896 - 1944
.............          +Marie Vera Kuzova  1907 - 1992
.......... 3        Alice (Liese) Beykovský     1898 - 1944
.............          +Rudolf (Rudi) Frank 1891 - 1963
.......... 3        Ruzena Beykovský    1900 - 1983
.............          +Bruno Emanuel Fürth      1888 - 1951
.... 2   Siegfried Beykovský  1867 - 1926
........          +Adele Reitler 1878 - 1929
.... 2   Adele Beykovský      1871 - 1918
```

....   +Samuel Krasa   1860 - 1934
.... 3   Franz Krasa   1893 - 1972
....   +Waltrante Anna Henriette Huber   1914 -
.... 3   Liese Krasa   1896 - 1977
....   +Karl Mayer 1888 - 1941
.... 2   Richard Beykovský   1873 –

DESCENDANTS OF ANNA BEYKOVSKÝ-2003

1 Anna Beykovský 1875 - 1951
  +Viktor Dr. Pick 1871 –
 2 Joseph Erich Pick 1898 - 1971
  +Doris Madeline Endel 1909 – 2000
  3 Patricia Pick 1938 -
   +Roy Howard Trumbull 1939 -
    4 Erica Ilana Trumbull 1967 –
    4 Jason Stearns August 27, 1963
     5 Isaac Arnold Trumbull-Stearns
January 24, 2004
    4 David Ian Trumbull 1969 -
     +Regina Harrison-Bayless 1967 -
     5 Loveday Harrison Trumbull 2000 -
     5 Miles Harrison Trumbull 2003 –

  3 Viktor Michael Pick 1936 -
   +Nancy Quin 1937 -
   4 Leslie Alice Pick 1961 -
    +Michael William Moore 1959 -
   4 Christopher Michael Pick 1963 -
    +Deirdre Elizabeth King 1960 -
    5 Eric Michael Pick 1992 -
    5 Elaine Ann Pick 1994 -
   *2nd Wife of Viktor Michael Pick:
   +Patricia (Patti) Madden Thomas 1946 –

 2 Adele Pick 1901 - 1984
  +JuDr. Vitezslav Kersch 1898 – 1944
  3 Emil Viktor Kersch 1922 – 1944
  3 Emmy Angelica Kersch Berger 1924 - 2000
   +Albert Pepitone 1922 - Lives in USA
   4 Leslie Angelica Pepitone 1954 -
   4 Jessica Pepitone 1956 -

4   Andrea Pepitone   1958 -

4   Viktor Pepitone   1960 – 1992

3 Ludwig Sebastian Kersch   1927 - Lives in Georgia US

*2nd Husband of Adele Pick:
+Fritz Berger - 1968
*3rd Husband of Adele Pick:
+Henry H. Hausner   1901 – 1995
*2nd Wife of [1] JuDr. Vitezslav Kersch:

+Anna Sucha b: September 25, 1904 d: January 27, 2001

DESCENDANTS OF JOSEF BEYKOVSKÝ

1   Josef Beykovský b: December 12, 1834   d: September 25, 1921
        +Louisa Dubský b: September 12, 1843   d: May 09, 1909
    2 Gustav Beykovský   b: December 06, 1864 d: November, 14 1929
        +Luise Glück   b: December 28, 1867   d: Abt. 1929
        3   Otto Beykovský b: April 16, 1896 d: Abt. 1916
        3   Karl Beykovský b: April 23, 1897
        3   Viktor Josef Beykovský   b: March 21, 1902   d: August 17, 1975
            +Gabriele Kende b: September 12, 1901   d: January 05, 1994
            4 [2] Jirko (George) Harry Beykovský b: August 22, 1931
            +Barbara Ann Hathaway   b: February 20, 1939
                5   Steven Craig Beykovský b: January 22, 1960
                5   [1] Edward Vincent Beykovský   b: September 24, 1962
                +Evelyn Denise White   b: September 05, 1964
                *2nd Wife of [1] Edward Vincent Beykovský
                +Kathleen Jo Eastlick   b: February 06, 1960
                    6   Amy Lynn Beykovský   b: April 16, 1982
                    6   April Dawn Beykovský   b: April 16, 1982
                       + Aaron Charles Marvin   b: November 20, 1981
                    6   Adam Brice Beykovský   b: March 29, 1984
                    6   Alyssa Ann Beykovský   b: July 03, 1989
                    6   Ashley May Beykovský   b: September 10, 1993
                5   Paul Joseph Beykovský   b: November 24, 1964
                +Debbie Louise Jones Dobbelaar   b: July 01, 1962
                    6   Brendan Joseph Beykovský b: August 04, 1991

6 Nathan Drew Beykovský b: July 21, 1993

*2nd Wife of [2] Jirko Harry Beykovský
+Helene Marie Watkins b: February 26, 1943
4 Tomas Jan Beykovský b: February 19, 1936

+Catherine Keir Layton Irwin b: January 17, 1940

5 Andrew Viktor Dr. Beykovský b: November 12, 1964

+Kyra Olga Yurrita Gaitan b: May 11, 1967

 6. William Enrique Beykovský b: December 22, 2001
 1. Fernando Enrique Beykovský b: June 22, 2005
 6 David Enrique Beykovský May 2, 2007

5 Karen Gabriele Beykovský b: June 28, 1966

+Jerry Hazbun b: September 28, 1963
 6 Catherine Hazbun b: January 29, 1991
 6 Jessica Hazbun b: October 29, 1994
 6 Joshua Hazbun b: April 03, 1998

5 Jan Kevin Beykovský b: August 20, 1968

+Maria-Isabel Batres b: June 21, 1972
 6 Kevin Alexander Beykovský b: September 28, 1997

 6 Christopher Thomas Beykovský b: July 26, 2002

2 Vilem Beykovský b: August 22, 1867 d: January 27, 1942

+Marie Rosenbaum b: September 11, 1880 d: Abt. 1942
3 Anna Beykovský b: January 30, 1902 d: Abt. 1944
+Mudr. Adolf Elsner b: April 22, 1899 d: July 30, 1948

4 Hanna Renee Elsner b: January 26, 1926

+Jiri Ing. Fuchs b: April 04, 1921 d: January 24, 1977
 5 Michael Vilem Ing. Fuchs b: September 18, 1946

+Dagmar Pavlas b: August 14, 1946

6   Daniel Fuchs   b: March 10, 1969

+Jennifer Hughes Horner b: March 17, 1967

7 Hailey Witcroft Fuchs b: August 05, 2001

7 Samantha Kathryn Fuchs b: July 31, 2003

6   Veronika Fuchs b: March 11, 1976

+Timothy Michael Quinn b: November 10, 1973

5 [3] Martin Jan Ing. Fuchs   b: January 15, 1949

+Iva Ing. Polakova   d: November 1975

*2nd Wife of [3] Martin Jan Ing. Fuchs:

+Jana Smotlachova   b: March 21, 1951

6   Tereza Fuchs   b: July 27, 1979

+Petr Kravar   b: January 26, 1979

6   Helena Fuchs   b: May 05, 1983

5   Katerina Anna Ing. Fuchs b: July 02, 1950

5   Jana Barbora Ing. Fuchs b: October 17, 1955

+Martin Kucera b: December 06, 1953 d: August 20, 2004

6   Jan Kucera   b: 9/19/1988

6   Matej Kucera   b: August 27, 1990

3   Frantisek Beykovský   b: April 10, 1916 d: Abt. 1942

3   Jenik Jirik Beykovský   b: December 22, 1918   d: Abt. 1942

2   Otto Beykovský, Dr.   b: September 22, 1870   d: March 12, 1935

+ Hermina Kraus b: Dec 26, 1875 d: Dec 18, 1943

3   Arnos Bedrich Beykovský b: Aug 22, 1918 d: Dec 18, 1943

2   Ana Beykovský   b: September 15, 1875   d: January 28, 1951

+Viktor Dr. Pick b: February 05, 1871

3   Joseph Erich Pickb: June 09, 1898 d: April 19, 1971

+Doris Madeline Endel   b: November 11, 1909   d:
March 30, 2000

4   Patricia Pick   b: May 04, 1938
+Roy Howard Trumbull   b: November 28, 1939
            5   Erica Ilana Trumbull   b: August
26, 1967

+Jason Stearns
            6   Isaac Arnold Stearns b:
January 24, 2004

            5   David Ian Trumbull   b: April 19,
1969

+Regina Harrison-Bayless b: August 14, 1967

            6 Loveday Harrison Trumbull   b:
January 20, 2000

            6   Miles Harrison Trumbull b:
May 06, 2003

4   [4] Viktor Michael Pick   b: March 12, 1936

+Nancy Quin   b: December 03, 1937
            5   Leslie Alice Pick b: July 09, 1961
+Michael William Moore b: June 20, 1959
            5   Christopher Michael Pick b: November
16, 1963

+Deirdre Elizabeth King   b: May 20, 1960
            6   Eric Michael Pick   b: August
30, 1992

            6   Elaine Ann Pick b: May 12,
1994

*2nd Wife of [4] Viktor Michael Pick:
+Patricia (Patti) Madden Thomas   b: December 06, 1946

3   [5] Adele Pick   b: September 07, 1901   d: November
04, 1984

+JuDr. Vitezslav Kersch   b: September 26, 1898   d:
Abt. 1944

4   Emil Viktor Kersch   b: May 02, 1922 d:
Abt. 1944

4 Emmy Angelica Kersch Berger   b: January 08, 1924 d:
August 22, 2000

+Albert Pepitone b: Abt. 1922
            5   Leslie Angelica Pepitone b: Abt. 1954

            5   Jessica Pepitone b: Abt. 1956
            5   Andrea Pepitone b: Abt. 1958

          5   Viktor Pepitone   b: Abt. 1960d: Abt.
1992
          4   Ludwig Sebastian Kersch b: October 12, 1927

*2nd Husband of [5] Adele Pick:
+Fritz Berger   d: Abt. 1968
*3rd Husband of [5] Adele Pick:
+Henry H. Hausner   b: January 06, 1901   d: April
07, 1995

DESCENDANTS OF L. POLLAK AUGUST 12, 2005

1 Löbl Pollak b: Abt. 1790 d:February 6, 1861
+Marie Volfova b: Abt. 1795 d:August 5, 1880
 2 Elisa Pollak b: Abt. 1821
 2 Philip Pollak b: Abt. 1822 d:May 12, 1890
 2 Emanuel Pollak b: Abt. 1823 d:April 4, 1884
 2 Jakub Löbl Pollak b: September 19, 1824 d: October 07, 1882
  +Rosalie (Ruzena) Beykovský b: August 16, 1831 d: September 12, 1891
  3 Aloisa (Luiza) Pollak b: July 21, 1856 d: July 18, 1911
   +William Kreitner b: December 10, 1848
  3 [1] Klara Pollak b: March 09, 1857 d: April 19, 1916
   +Adalbert Oplatek b: Abt. 1846
   *2nd Husband of [1] Klara Pollak:
   +Hans (Heinrich) Schiller b: Abt. 1863
  3 Berta Pollak b: November 07, 1858 d: March 01, 1934
   +Alfred Gärtner b: January 27, 1857 d: June 30, 1942
   4 Vally (Valerie) Gärtner b: July 17, 1885 d: October 10, 1939
    +Karel Back b: April 20, 1881 d: September 10, 1939
    5 Jiri Back b: August 12, 1909 d: January 21, 1945
    5 Otto Back b: November 06, 1912 d: Abt. 1987
     +Eva Melzer b: Abt. 1913 d: Abt. 1989
     6 Tomas Back b: Abt. 1947
     6 Mary Anna Back b: Abt. 1949
    5 Arnost Back b: September 04, 1914 d: Abt. 1999
     +Olga Back
    5 Evzen Back b: November 24, 1917 d: February 1943

4   Richard Gärtnerb: September 01, 1886 d: March 07, 1943

+Elsa (Eliska) Rubichek   b: Abt. 1893   d: March 07, 1943

4   Vilos (Vilem) Gärtner   b: October 16, 1887 d: 1942

+Julie Hermann   b: June 04, 1905 d: March 07, 1944
          5   Harry Gärtner   b: June 02, 1925 d: March 07, 1944

4 Gustav (Gustl) Gärtner b: December 15, 1888 d: February 13, 1983

+Olga (Oly) Winternitz   b: May 14, 1900 d: January 06, 1986

          5 Erika Eva Gärtner b: September 03, 1921
          +Dr. Donald Alexander Fraser b: January 23, 1918d: Nov 29, 2003

          6   Steven Donald Fraser   b: March 23, 1956

          6 Spruce Sandra Fraser   b: Sep. 27, 1958
Lives in St Louis, MO   +James
Hing Kuen Yip   b: September 21, 1951
                              7 Chadwick Fraser Yip   b: October 06, 1995

          4   Erick Gärtner   b: April 05, 1890 d: Abt. 1943
          +Edith Roubichek   b: January 20, 1903   d: February 06, 1984

Lives in California

          5 [2] Stephan Gärtner   b: July 29, 1929

          +Vera Luz Koknova   b: Abt. 1930
                    6   David Gärtner   b: Abt. 1966
                                      + Sandi Bendel
                    7.   Kaela Gärtner   b: Abt 2001
7   Jadon Gärtner b: Abt 2003

                    6   Lia Gärtner   b: Abt. 1972

                    +Sunjya Schweig
                    7   Kaia Schweig   b: Abt. 2002

                    7   Kiva Schweig   b: Abt. 2005

          *2nd Wife of [2] Stephan Gärtner:
          +Carolyn Hall b: Feb. 08, 1934 - d: Sep. 17, 2005

          5   Hans JuDr. Gärtner   b: January 04, 1936

          +Frida Gärtner   b: Abt. 1936

6 Erica Dr. Gärtner b: Abt. 1956

+Max MUDr. Toman
  7 Melanie Toman b:
February 27, 1987
  7 Camilla Toman b:
Abt. 1992
4 Eugene (Evzen) Gärtner b: April 05, 1890 d:
Abt. 1943

+Olga Holzner b: Abt. 1893 d: Abt. 1943
  5 Justina Gärtner b: February 09, 1928

4 Hedda (Hedvika)Gärtner b: September 01, 1892
d: Abt. 1942
 +Emil Epstein b: January 07, 1883 d: Abt. 1942
  5 Erich Epstein b: March 21, 1915
d: Abt. 1942
  5 Lily Epstein b: March 14, 1917
d: May 2004
 +Rudolf Holzner b: Abt. 1904 d: Abt. 1990
  6 Rachel Holzner Abt 1946

  +Gad Negbi Abt 1945

  7 Alon Negbi b: Abt.
1972
   + Sigal
Ruach Abt 1972
   8 Roi Negbi
Abt 2001
   8 Nadav
Negbi Abt 2003*
   8 Tal Negbi
Abt 2003* Twins
  7 Yael Negbi b: Abt. 1974
   + Yaniv
Rosner Abt 1974
   8 Shira
Rosner Abt 2004
  7 Erez Negbi b: Abt.
1976
  7 Oren Negbi b: Abt.
1981
4 Ada (Adela) Gärtner b: April 12, 1893 d:
April 04, 1952

+Alfred Ing Schwarz   b: April 20, 1886 d: February 16, 1957

    5   Hedvika Schwarz b: April 11, 1919 d: Abt. 1998

+Jaroslav JUDr. Zeman   b: Abt. 1907 d: September 07, 1984

      6   Maria Zeman   b: November 19, 1947

+Petr Uhlir   b: Abt. 1947
       7   Jan Uhlir   b: Abt. 1973

       7   Petr Uhlir   b: Abt. 1976

      6   Karel Zeman   b: December 07, 1949

+Dorota Klouska b: Abt. 1949
       7   Jacub Zeman   b: Abt. 1975

       7   Marie Zeman   b: Abt. 1981

    5   Eva Schwarz   b: April 25, 1922
+Vladimir Liska b: June 10, 1926
      6   Jan Liska   b: May 04, 1949

+Jana Vratna   b: June 12, 1954
       7   Petr Liska   b: September 20, 1978

       7   Tomas Liska   b: November 05, 1981

      6   Jiri Liska   b: August 27, 1953

+Irena Jehlicek   b: August 07, 1957

       7   Mariana Liska   b: June 07, 1981

       7   Jan Liska   b: November 01, 1982

       7   Karolina Liska   b: December 12, 1984
    3   Gottlieb (Bohumil) Pollak b: February 19, 1860 d: June 08, 1881
    3   Leopold (Poldi) Pollak   b: May 07, 1861 d: Abt. 1911
+Kamila Kohn   b: March 28, 1870   d: Abt. 1939
    4   Hana Pollak   b: Abt. 1893   d: Abt. 1944
+Max Ing. Stein b: March 10, 1880   d: December 07, 1943

5   Karel Stein   b: Abt. 1921 d: Abt. 1940

5   Jirka Stein   b: Abt. 1922

4   Helena Pollak   b: October 07, 1896 d: Abt. 1943

+Franta Brummel b: Abt. 1900   d: Abt. 1943

5   Jirka Brummel   b: Abt. 1928 d: Abt. 1943

4   Else (Eliska) Pollak   b: December 24, 1897 d: Abt. 1970

+Dr Rudolf (Rudi) Kraus b: Abt. 1897   d: Abt. 1995

5   [3] Hans (John-Yochanan) Kraus   b: Abt. 1929

+Sylvia Kraus

6   Gad Kraus   b: Abt. 1957

+Rachel Kraus   b: Abt. 1959

7   Netta Kraus b: Abt. 1985

7   Haggai Kraus   b: Abt. 1989

7   Yahel Kraus b: Abt. 1992

6   Dina Kraus   b: Abt. 1960

+Ronny Drori

7   Dafna Drori b: Abt. 1986

7   Sheera Drori   b: Abt. 1992

7   Guy Drori b: Abt. 1997

6   David Kraus   b: Abt. 1963

+Claudia Kraus

*2nd Wife of [3] Hans (John-Yochanan) Kraus:

+Miriam Kraus

6   Maya Kraus   b: Abt. 1980

5   [4] Dora (Dolly) Kraus   b: Abt. 1930

Lives in Israel

+Josef (Pepik) Asherman   d: Abt. 1967

6   Ilan Asherman   b: Abt. 1960

+Michal Asherman

Abt. 1990

Abt. 1993

b: Abt. 1998

Kraus
Luz   d: Abt. 1995

Abt. 1940

1943

1943

20, 1952

January 20, 1952

December 10, 1976

Drori:

26, 1952

07, 1988

February 04, 1990

1958

April 19, 1997

January 11, 1999

7   Alon Asherman   b:

7   Adi Asherman   b:

6   Ami Asherman   b: Abt. 1962

7   Na'ama Asherman

*2nd Husband of [4] Dora (Dolly)
                               +Yair
Hanus (Hans) Pollak   b: June 25, 1900 d:

+Rosa Pollak   b: Abt. 1900   d: Abt. 1943
5   Petr Pollak   b: Abt. 1927d: Abt.

5   Stepan Pollak   b: Abt. 1931d: Abt.

Karel Pollak   b: June 15, 1903 d: Abt. 1945
+Alice Pollak   b: Abt. 1907
5   [5] Hanka Pollak b: Abt. 1931
+Israel Ben-Zvi   b: Abt. 1922   d: Abt. 1971
           6   Rami Ben-Zvi   b: January

*2nd Husband of [5] Hanka Pollak:
+Chaim Drori   b: Abt. 1930
           6   [6] Ram Ben-Zvi Drori   b:

           +Lea Ben-Zvi
           7   Haj Drori   b:

           *2nd Wife of [6] Ram Ben-Zvi

           +Ada Drori   b: January

           7   Roni Drori   b: April

           7   Gal Drori   b:

           6   Doron Drori   b: June 05,

+Carina Landquist
           7   Dan Landquist   b:

           7   Alma Landquist   b:

6 Nir Drori b: June 05, 1958

+Orna Drori b: May 03, 1962

7 Nittay Drori b: November 26, 1993

7 Carmel Drori b: October 01, 1996

6 Tamar Drori b: February 17, 1965

+Ilan Lhncor b: April 30, 1957

7 Yumal Drori b: August 19, 1996

7 Amit Drori b: June 01, 1998

7 Noa Drori b: April 19, 2001

3 Emil (Emilian) Pollak b: January 06, 1863 d: Abt. 1939

+Karla Fuchs b: April 06, 1874 d: Abt. 1936

3 Heinrich (Jindrich) Pollak b: August 04, 1864 d: Abt. 1938

+Henrietta Bohring b: Abt. 1866
4 Rudolf Pollak b: Abt. 1901 d: Abt. 1920
4 Elisabeth Pollak b: Abt. 1904 d: Abt. 1932
4 Wolfgang Werner Pollak b: Abt. 1911

3 Hugo Pollak b: October 18, 1866 d: March 11, 1935

+Thekla Lichtenstadt b: September 04, 1871 d: Abt. 1939

4 Hans Gunther Pollak b: May 03, 1894 d: August 24, 1983

+Lisl (Elizabeth) Sofer b: March 23, 1902 d: October 29, 2001

5 Grace Diane Polk b: July 01, 1941
Lives in NY

4 Mimi (Zdenka) Pollak b: Abt. 1895
+Ernst Orenstein b: Abt. 1890 d: Abt. 1960
5 Otto Orenstein b: Abt. 1920 d: Abt. 1994

5 Tony Orenstein b: Abt. 1922 d: Abt. 2000

4 George Pollak b: Abt. 1902 d: Abt. 1938

3 Ottokar Ludwig Dr. Pollak b: March 10, 1870 d: Abt. 1915

+Gertrude Princess b: Abt. 1870

2   Johanna Pollak   b: Abt. 1825

DESCENDANTS OF SAMUEL BEYKOVSKÝ 2005

Samuel Beykovský 1719-1809
   +Anna 1719 -1793
         +Katharina Polacek 1719- (second wife of Samuel)
1 Herman Beykovský   1758 –   Ancestors of Helena and Karel Bejkovsky
1 Anna Beykovský   1759 –
1 Magdalena Beykovský 1761 -
1 Bernard Beykovský   1763 -1830
         +Sara Pozer   1770 -
     2   Abraham Beykovský   1801 - 1802
     2   Lidmila Beykovský   1801 -
     2   Jakub Beykovský 1804 - 1881
         +Anna Baumann 1808 - 1884
     3   Rosalie (Ruzena) Beykovský   1831 - 1891
         +Jakob Löbl Pollak   1824 - 1882
         4   Aloisa (Luiza) Pollak   1856 - 1911
           +William Kreitner   1848 -
         4   [1] Klara Pollak 1857 - 1916
           +Adalbert Oplatek   1846 -
           *2nd Husband of [1] Klara Pollak:
           +Hans (Heinrich) Schiller 1842
           4 Berta Pollak   1858 – 1934
Spruce Fraser and
           +Alfred Gärtner 1857 - 1942   Stephan
Gärtner ancestor
         4   Gottlieb (Bohumil) Pollak 1860 - 1881
         4   Leopold (Poldi) Pollak   1861 - 1911
           +Kamila Kohn   1870 - 1939
         4   Emil (Emilian) Pollak   1863 - 1939
           +Karla Fuchs   1874 - 1936
         4   Heinrich (Jindrich) Pollak 1864 - 1938
           +Henrietta Bohring   1866 -
         4   Hugo Pollak   1866 – 1935   Grace
Polk ancestor
           +Thekla Lichtenstadt   1871 - 1939
         4   Ottokar Ludwig Dr. Pollak 1870 - 1915
           +Gertrude Princess   1870 -
     3   Adolf Beykovský 1833 – 1871   Peter Lowe ancestor
         +Rosa Fischl
     3   Josef Beykovský 1834 – 1921
         +Louisa Dubsky 1843 - 1909

        4   Gustav Beykovský   1864 -   George
Beykovský ancestor

                   +Luise Glück   1867 - 1929
        4   Vilem Beykovský   1867 – 1942   Hanna
Fuchs ancestor

                   +Marie Sara Rosenbaum   1880 - 1942
        4   Otto Beykovský 1870 - 1935
                   +Hermine Kraus 1875 - 1943
        4   Anna Beykovský 1875 – 1951   Pat Trumbull
ancestor

                   +Viktor Dr. Pick 1871 -
        3   Nathan Beykovský   1842 – 1842 (Maybe still-born)
        2   Rosarie Beykovský   1807 -
        2   No-name Beykovský   1808 –1808 (Maybe still-born)
        2   Josef Beykovský   1809 -
        2   Salomon Beykovský   1811 -
        2   Mojzis Beykovský   1813 -1878
        2   Anna Beykovský   1814 -
        2   Marie Beykovský 1816 –
1 Lazar Beykovský 1765 -

DESCENDANTS OF VILEM BEYKOVSKÝ

```
1   Vilem Beykovský         1867 - 1942
     +Marie Rosenbaum       1880 - 1942
   2  Anna Beykovský 1902 - 1944
 +Mudr. Adolf Elsner  1899 - 1948
   3  Hanna Renee Elsner      1926 -
              + Jiri Fuchs      1921 - 1977
       4 Michael Vilem Fuchs     1946 –Lives in Boston
              +Dagmar Pavlas  1946 -
                      5        Daniel Fuchs        1969 -
                      +Jennifer Hughes Horner  1967 -
                      6 Hailey Witcroft Fuchs    2001 -
                      6 Samantha Kathryn Fuchs 2003 -
                      5        Veronika Fuchs     1976 -
                      +Timothy Michael Quinn  1973 -
       4 Martin Jan Fuchs        1949 -
              + Iva Polakova    - 1975
              *2nd Wife of Martin Jan Fuchs:
              +Jana Smotlachova         1951 -
                      5        Tereza Fuchs        1979 -
                      +Petr Kravar       1979 -
                      5        Helena Fuchs        1983 -
       4      Katerina Anna Fuchs        1950 -
       4      Jana Barbora Fuchs        1955 -
              +Martin Kucera  1953 -2004
                      5        Jan Kucera          1988 -
                      5        Matej Kucera        1990 -
   2  Frantisek Beykovský      1916 - 1942
   2  Jenik Jirik Beykovský     1918 – 1942
```

Research Notes:

- The abbreviation "Abt" or "About" next to names indicate an approximate date of birth or death. I might not have the exact date.
- I have found several ways to spell our surname: Bakovsky, Bejkovsky, Beykovski, Beykovský, and, Beykowsky. I mostly use Beykovský. One family used Bakovsky when immigrating to USA. To explain the various spellings, one theory is that the scribes who wrote the entries in the archives had a Germanic background as during the Austrian Hungarian Empire reign, or a Czech scribes as when the Czechoslovak Republic was formed after WWI.
- The accent or tilde on the last " _ý_ " of our surname appears on many hand written documents and also on my father's and other our ancestor signatures. I use this form when signing my name. In modern times, when the name is typewritten, the accent has been dropped.
- In my father's generation and before, after a woman married a Beykovský she carried the name Beykovsková, and if they had a daughter she would be called Beykovská. This has been of common usage also of other surnames in the Czech language.

Lightning Source UK Ltd.
Milton Keynes UK
UKHW02182508032
359976UK00019B/394